SHORT CUTS

INTRODUCTIONS TO FILM STUDIES

THE GANGSTER FILM

FATAL SUCCESS IN AMERICAN CINEMA

RON WILSON

WALLFLOWER

LONDON and NEW YORK

A Wallflower Press Book

Wallflower Press is an imprint of
Columbia University Press
Publishers Since 1893
New York, Chichester, West Sussex
cup.columbia.edu

Cover image: *Goodfellas* (1990) © Warner Bros/Dirck Halstead

A complete CIP record is available from the Library of Congress

ISBN 978-0-231-17207-3 (pbk. : alk. paper)
ISBN 978-0-231-85067-4 (e-book)

p 10 9 8 7 6 5 4 3 2 1

CONTENTS

ACKNOWLEDGEMENTS

I would like to express my gratitude to the Department of Film and Media Studies at the University of Kansas, and particularly Dr. Tamara Falicov, the department Chair, for allowing the opportunity to teach several courses where I initially engaged many of the ideas expressed in this volume. I would also like to thank the immensely talented and industrious students in my graduate writing course who, time and again, were subject to hearing about writing examples such as paragraph structure, proper citation format, integration of sources etc that I was currently working on in drafts of this manuscript. Special thanks go to David Sutera, who helped with the images. Words cannot express my gratitude to Yoram Allon, Commissionng Editor at Wallflower Press, for his professional expertise, patience and fervent belief in this project. And finally I owe a heartfelt thanks to all of the staff at Wallflower Press in helping to develop and guide the manuscript through the publication process.

INTRODUCTION

The opening sequence of *Bugsy* (1991) is a perfect synthesis of some of the thematic concerns of the American gangster film. Within its short seven-minute duration director Barry Levinson is able to incorporate not only the delineation of character traits associated with its gangster protagonist Bugsy Siegel, but also a major concern of the gangster film itself – the power of consumption. The sequence begins with a medium shot of the outside of a house in the dead of winter. A voice-over conversation informs us that a husband/father is leaving on a business trip. We next see a car travelling along a road in long shot and hear its occupant indulging in elocution lessons ('Twenty dwarves took turns doing hand stands on the carpet. Twenty dwarves...'). Inter-cutting these short scenes with the credits themselves, Levinson then shows the man in a clothing store buying shirts. When the salesman addresses him as 'Mr. Siegel' a bystander informs his wife, 'That's Bugsy Siegel'. It is at that point that we finally see a close-up of the man's face as he has clearly heard the remark. Overshadowed by the silhouettes of store mannequins in the window who loom threateningly over the scene, 'Bugsy' admonishes and verbally intimidates the man's reference to 'something that crawls around in the dirt' rather than his real name of Benjamin ('It's in the Bible').

The following scene is in a hotel lobby where Bugsy Siegel picks up an attractive girl in an elevator ('If we make love it will be the only time'). This is followed by an interior shot of the hotel room where clothes are strewn over a chair and we overhear the sounds of lovemaking in progress. The next scene is inside an automobile on a rain-soaked street; the people inside are presumably Siegel's employers and are discussing a business problem that needs to be taken care of, Siegel taking care of the problem by killing the front-operator of a bookie joint who has been 'stealing the shirt off my back' then follows this. Before shooting him at point blank range, Siegel politely informs him that it is 'just business, like selling insurance or importing dresses'. The short sequence highlights the power of the gangster in matters of family, sex, conspicuous consumption, intimidation, and killing. In so doing it also showcases our fascination with a character seemingly beyond the law and the bounds of morality. Ostensibly showing a man simply going to work we shortly discover what that work is and how successfully he performs it.

The gangster film presents a distorted vision of the American success story – where the gangster avoids the hard road to success by simply taking what he wants when he wants it. According to Robert Warshow, 'the story of his career is a nightmare inversion of the values of ambition and opportunity'; the gangster, though crude, is never inarticulate and can state definitely what he wants, 'to take over the North Side, to own a hundred suits, to be Number One' (1962: 106, 107). Yet it would be a mistake to think that this is the only thing that the gangster represents or the only way he is depicted in American film. The gangster was presented differently at different historical junctures and circumstances. Even within the so-called 'classical gangster films' of the early 1930s the gangster was manifest in various genres from musicals to comedies. More important is how the representation of the gangster in American film is closely associated with his topicality outside of film. As historian Jonathan Munby notes 'the gangster film changed over time subject to the multiple determinations of generic evolution, moral intervention, and the need to remain topical in a rapidly changing world' (1999: 4). Indicative of this change is the etymology of the word itself.

According to the OED the initial use of the word 'gangster' occurred in 1884 in the *Cincinnati Commercial Gazette* in the following entry: 'They have a candidate for the Presidency, and his name is Grover Cleveland, the creature of a combination of gangsters and cranks.' In another instance the *Columbus Evening Dispatch* in 1884 reported: 'The gangster may play all sorts of pranks with the ballot box, but in its own good time the latter will get even by kicking the gangster in the gutter.' The word usage reveals several things that are important to bear in mind: first, the word 'gangster' is clearly a derogatory term indicating an individual or individuals who are beneath contempt, and more significantly, it is a topical term connected with actual events by virtue of its use in a newspaper article. Moreover, it is also related to an urban environment, as well as to a type of strong-arm behaviour that would become commonplace in turn-of-the-century American politics. This brief etymology of the term is significant in that it lays the foundation for a film genre that originates in the early 1900s and remains popular to this day.

The gangster film, unlike other film genres – such as the western, the action-adventure film, the science fiction film, and others – is the only genre whose nomenclature is centered on an individual, rather than a concept. The gangster as an individual becomes central to the genre itself and its significance, particularly to American culture and values. This becomes evident in some of the film titles alone: *Musketeers of Pig Alley* (1912), *Little Caesar* (1931), *Scarface* (1932), *Bonnie and Clyde* (1968), *The Godfather* (1972), and *Bugsy*, as well as a host of others. In addition, whereas many film genres have their locus in originating literature, Mary Shelley's *Frankenstein* (both horror and science fiction), Owen Wister's *The Virginian* (the western), Raymond Chandler's *The Big Sleep* (*film noir*), by contrast, gangster film narratives originate from the headlines, topical events, and true-crime narratives of newspapers and tabloid publications. Warner Bros.' head of production at the time of the initial gangster cycle of the early 1930s, Darryl F. Zanuck, wanted to produce stories 'that were timely and which would touch upon subjects vital to the public' (Custen 1997: 131). The 'timely' stories of 1930–31 concerned gangsterism that flaunted the 18th Amendment – Prohibition; and Al Capone, who flaunted the American success story. The gangster would become a subversive figure both on- and off-screen, but whereas the real-life gangster is ultimately simply a criminal, the on-screen gangster becomes something more – an imaginative idea, a metaphor for individualism, success, the Depression, the syndicate, post-war alienation, or family values.

The gangster film remains popular primarily because it is easily adaptable to reflect contemporaneous concerns. The gangster protagonist can be seen in films based on contemporary true-crime non-fiction such as *Goodfellas* (1990) through to the likes of Walter White, whose criminal activity as survival practice and ultimate hubris is the narrative thrust in the popular AMC series, *Breaking Bad* (2008–2013). The gangster remains a popular character in American film because of his relationship to outlaw culture and the meanings associated with that culture.

Genre Criticism and the Gangster Film

The gangster film was one of the first film genres to be the focus of both popular and scholarly writing in early genre criticism. Along with the western it established a methodological approach to film genre criticism from its aesthetic qualities to structural analysis. In addition, the gangster film provided a means for evaluating American cultural attitudes and values through its critique of individualism and the myth of the dream of success. More recently, gangster film criticism has focused on historical and cultural analysis rather than ideological perspectives with an emphasis on Hollywood studio production practices and the fragmentation of the genre into specific cycles of films. This short survey of gangster film criticism allows for an understanding of the ways the genre has been viewed as an important American genre within the context of film studies.

Popular criticism of the gangster film begins with Robert Warshow's seminal essay, 'The Gangster as Tragic Hero', first published in *The Parisian Review* in 1948. Warshow contends that the gangster is a product of the modern age and is representative of the urban milieu that has surpassed American agrarian life. More specifically the gangster is a metaphor for 'that part of the American psyche which rejects the qualities and demands of modern life' (1962: 130). For Warshow the gangster is essentially an instrument for critiquing 'Americanism' itself, particularly the American work ethic. The gangster's steady, upward progress is typically followed by a precipitous fall – in essence the gangster is doomed because of his obligation to succeed. Though the essay is restrictive in its miniscule sampling of gangster films it is the cornerstone of aesthetic and ideological examinations of the genre.

The numerous 'little books' published in the early 1970s best represent early pre-academic criticism of the gangster film. According to Mark Betz these physically small ('usually around 18cm x 13.5cm') film studies series were intended for a general readership consisting primarily of cinephiles and pre-date more scholarly approaches to film. The little books generally covered a single topic such as 'The Films of Howard Hawks' or 'The American Film Musical'. These historical surveys were characterised by their filmographies and reference material rather than in-depth analysis. For example *The Gangster Film* (1970) by John Baxter is primarily an encyclopedic reference to historical figures and events, actors, directors, and writers associated with the genre. John Gabree's *Gangsters: From Little Caesar to The Godfather* (1973) presents a brief historical survey of the genre from the early 1930s to the earlt 1970s. Most of these texts are broadly focused so as to include not only the gangster film but also crime films in general, including *film noir*. Colin McArthur's *Underworld U.S.A.* (1972) is the first in-depth examination of the gangster/thriller genre and 'constituted a groundbreaking exercise in making visible and delineating the genre' (Gledhill 1985: 86). Sketching out the iconography and conventions of the gangster film, McArthur then turns his attention to several directors associated with the genre. In this way the book reflects an auteur-structuralist viewpoint that was in vogue at the time and provides a springboard to the formal genre criticism to follow.

From 1977 to 1983 formal genre criticism established a more academic approach to film studies. Influenced by literary theory, particularly structuralism, film genre criticism along with auteurism was the standard of film scholarship. More detailed historical analysis of the genre as well as broadening the defining characteristics of genre within historical parameters provided concentrated studies of westerns, musicals, and gangster films. An examination of the genre's basic structure contributed to an understanding of deeper meanings within the genre itself, especially social meanings. Within gangster film criticism several notable works stand out.

Jack Shadoian's *Dreams and Dead Ends: The American Gangster Film*, first published in 1977, examines the basic structure of the gangster film as 'ready made for certain kinds of concerns' (2003: 4), concerns that Shadoian claims arise out of the contradictions of the 'American dream' of success and the urban environment that created the gangster. According to Shadoian, 'there is an inherent contradiction in American thought between America as a land of opportunity and the vision of a classless, democratic society' (2003: 6). The American promise of success and happiness is not always readily available to everyone. For Shadoian the 'gangster is a vehicle to expose this central problem of the American people' (ibid.). The aptly titled *Dreams and Dead Ends* presents a socio-cultural analysis of select gangster films that offer a unique critique of social and urban problems in American society.

Thomas Schatz's chapter on 'The Gangster Film' in *Hollywood Genres: Formulas, Filmmaking, and the Studio System* (1981) also examines the underlying structure of the gangster film as a reflection of the American ideal of the self-made man. Utilising the structuralist dichotomy of nature versus culture, Schatz argues that 'the mythology of the classic gangster film, like that of the western, concerns the transformation of nature into culture under the auspices of modern civilization' (1981: 82). The urban milieu of the gangster film represents a contested space 'where forces of social order and anarchy are locked in an epic and unending struggle' (1981: 83). This is reflected in the law-and-order/cops-and-robbers narratives that often dominate the genre. Serving a dual function, the urban environment represents an arena for physical action serving as an externalisation of the gangster persona and is also representative of social progress and destiny, which work to eradicate the gangster. Though the classic gangster cycle ended with the implementation of the Production Code in 1934, Schatz argues that this resulted in the numerous genre variations on the gangster in the late 1930s, including the gangster-as-cop and Cain-and-Abel varia-tions that often counterbalanced the gangster with a pro-social figure. This fragmentation of the genre is important in seeing how the gangster film survived by adapting itself to generic variants where the gangster himself becomes emblematic of hardened criminality.

Another examination of the genre that emphasised production history itself is Nick Roddick's *A New Deal in Entertainment: Warner Brothers in the 1930s* (1983). As its title suggests the book specifically examines the films of Warner Bros. during the Depression paying attention to production cycles such as newspaper pictures, historical films, and the gangster film. In this regard Roddick's approach is in line with André Bazin's notion of the 'genius of the system' (see Hillier 1985: 258) in regard to Hollywood studio production. According to Roddick, 'the kind of films which were made by Warners (and other studios) during the 1930s were strongly influenced by the economic and organizational system under which they were produced' (1983: 28). The gangster film was particularly economical because they were relatively cheap to make 'since they used contemporary dress, mini-mal sets (seedy restaurants, backroom offices, bland hotel rooms) and exteriors that rarely if ever called for anything other than the standing sets of the backlot' (1983: 99). This, coupled with their topicality 'straight from the headlines', made them particularly advantageous as part of Warners' production trend in the 1930s towards socially conscious movies aimed at a working-class audience. In many ways, Roddick's work pre-dates the historically specific studies that are representative of new genre criticism.

Influenced by the work of Rick Altman, Steve Neale, and Richard Maltby new genre criticism stresses a more focused approach to genres based on cultural studies and industrial history. Viewing film genres as a process that is continuously in flux, the cyclical nature of genres is distinguished as an important part of their variability. The historical reception of film genre cycles is often interweaved with the socio-cultural circumstances of production. *Inventing the Public Enemy: The Gangster in American Culture, 1918–1934* by David Ruth (1996) is indicative of the cultural studies approach to the gangster film. Situating his examination of the gangster specifically during Prohibition, Ruth argues that the gangster was a paragon of modern criminality who 'dramatized the development of an impersonal, highly organized, consumption-oriented urban society' (1996: 2). The gangster was less a reality than an image constructed by newspapers, the pulps, and films to comment on the corporate structure and consumption patterns of modern America. The cultural image of the gangster helped Americans 'master the changing social world' (ibid.) engendered by shifting business patterns based on an increasingly consumer-based society.

Another significant new genre critical approach to the gangster film focused on the ways the genre was fragmented by the implementation of the Production Code. Jonathan Munby's *Public Enemies, Public Heroes* (1999) argues that the gangster film and the censorship concerns associated with it represent attempts to contain its transgressive potential. Part of that transgressiveness was the gangster's ethnicity and 'otherness'. As Munby claims, 'in their blatant disregard for Prohibition and ironic mimicry of the laissez-faire capitalist "road to success," ethnic urban gangsters directly confronted the key moral and economic precepts associated with an ailing nativist order' (1999: 5). The early 1930s sound gangster film was particularly troublesome for moral guardians because it emphasised the gangsters ethnic identity through language. Munby views the Production Code as well as the Hays Office moratorium on gangster films in 1935 as initial attempts to reign in this popular figure. Hollywood studios countered through generic variations using the gangster in different types of crime films.

The exploration of the many incarnations of the gangster film is the subject of Fran Mason's *American Gangster Cinema: From Little Caesar to Pulp Fiction* (2002). He argues that although the gangster film 'may share a set of iconographic features and narrative patterns, these are multiple and cannot be reduced to those found in the classic narrative' (2002: xv). Film genre is best understood as a 'field of operations, which makes available a range of textual tropes, semiotic codes and narrative patterns ... rather than a reified codification of delimited conventions' (ibid.). The primary aim of the book is to study the variety and flexibility of the gangster film as a set of variations or sub-genres. Mason explores these variations through categories that include the post-Code gangster, syndicate and heist films, the post-classical gangster, as well as the postmodern gangster. By doing so he traces the generic development of the gangster film as a series of variations on a theme that is certainly a hallmark of film production.

Similarly Lee Grieveson, Esther Sonnet, and Peter Stanfield's *Mob Culture: Hidden Histories of the American Gangster Film* (2005) not only addresses generic variations, but also ethnicity, gender, and class in the genre. The primary aim of the book, the authors assert, is to 'show how the gangster figure is produced differently within historical intersections of cultural identity and the shifting cultural figurations of criminality' (2005: 1). By examining such film cycles as the syndicate films of the 1950s, the modern female films of the early 1930s, and even Chinatown Tong films of the 1920s and 1930s, as well as issues concerning masculinity and race, the book offers a different cultural perspective to some of the neglected American gangster films.

This brief survey of the literature surrounding the gangster film genre indicates how influential it is in genre study and American cinema. It also shows how extensive the gangster film is in terms of its product differentiation and how the mediated figure of the gangster changes over time. This transformation in the image is primarily based on historical and cultural circumstances that constantly re-mould the gangster into a figure that still addresses cultural concerns over criminality in modern society.

Purpose and Organisation of the Book

The aim of this volume is to trace the development of the gangster image in American cinema from its origins to the present in terms of characterisation, narrative structure, and motifs relevant to its historical and cultural specificity. Central to this study is the idea that film genres are not stable but fluid, adaptable, and cyclical. As Rick Altman notes:

> Genres are not just *post facto* categories ... but part of the constant category splitting/category creating dialectic that constitutes the history of types and terminology. Instead of imagining this process in terms of static classification, we might want to see it, in terms of regular alternation between an expansive principle – the creation of a new cycle – and a principle of contraction – the consolidation of a genre. (1999: 65)

The gangster film as genre, then, is consolidated through the numerous cycles and the variety of films within its corpus. To cite but one example, Michael Mann's *Public Enemies* (2009) with Johnny Depp as John Dillinger is an action-adventure based on the exploits of the notorious outlaw. For contemporary audiences it is a historical film that recreates the events of the crime wave of the mid-1930s within a cops-and-robbers narrative formula. Whereas during the mid-1930s a cycle of G-men films often used the Dillinger/Outlaw storyline as part of the narrative structure in a series of films focusing on federal agents. Though the name Dillinger was never used in these films, audiences would recognise the dramatic events nonetheless because of their proximity to the events themselves. The Dillinger/ Outlaw archetype would become a prominent one in the gangster film because it was able to adapt itself to the restrictions of the Production Code and allow studios to capitalise on the gangster image through a process of re-genrification. The process of genrification allows for the development of a genre through film cycles, genre-mixing, and historical reception.

This volume is organised by chapters that trace the development of the gangster film genre from its origins to the present by following major cultural and historical influences on the characterisation of the gangster image in American film. The first chapter, 'The Silent Era: From Gangs to Gangsters', is devoted to the evolution of the gangster in silent films from his beginnings as a street thug in Progressive-era crime films of the 1910s to the late 1920s cultural representation of the bootlegger as modern gangster. The second chapter, 'The Racketeer and the Outlaw', delineates two cultural archetypes of the gangster during the 1930s; one based on the historical figure of Al Capone, the other on the bandit image of outlaw John Dillinger. The suppression of the racketeer image by the enforcement of the Production Code and the subsequent moratorium on gangster films by Hollywood studios gave rise to the development of the outlaw archetype in the G-Man production cycle of the mid-1930s and other generic variations of the gangster in American film. The discussion of how historical events such as the Murder Incorporated trials of 1944 and Kefeauver hearings of 1951 further influenced the gangster film are the subject of chapter three, 'Murder, Incorporated: Post-war Developments of the Gangster Film'. The primary focus here is no longer the individual gangster but the syndicate – the corporate gangster. This chapter also considers the late 1950s retro-gangster film cycle that would influence nostalgic/historical representations of the gangster on film. Chapter five, '*La Famiglia*: Coppola, Scorsese and Gangster Ethnicity', concerns the depiction of the Italian-American experience in the genre in *The Godfather* films and *Goodfellas*. Francis Ford Coppola and Martin Scorsese are both central figures in the development of the gangster film in the post-Vietnam era and their films, particularly the image of *la famiglia* and the wise guys, have had a significant impact on American culture. The concluding chapter provides a short examination of the contemporary gangster film by looking at two production trends of the twenty-first century.

A central thematic motif running throughout this study is that the gangster film offers a twisted variation on the American success story and the idea of American individualism. As Robert Warshow points out, 'the gangster's whole life is an effort to assert himself as an individual, to draw himself out of the crowd, and he always dies *because* he is an individual; the final bullet thrusts him back, makes him, after all, a failure' (1962: 133). The image of the gangster may change over time, but he remains easily recognisable because of his desire for success and individuality – and perhaps this is the major reason for the continued popularity of the gangster in American film, because his desires often resonate with our own.

1   THE SILENT ERA: FROM GANGS TO GANGSTERS

In the heyday of the gangs the Bowery and Chatham Square constituted the crime district of the city, analogous to the flower market
or the garment district. There was a store on Elizabeth Street that
served as an underworld one-stop, selling pistols, brass knuckles,
stilettos, billy clubs of house manufacture with a lead slug in the
end, and its own design of blackjack, a six-inch leather bag filled
with shot, ending in a rope handle ... As it was said of the gangsters
of the era: 'When times are right, they go out every afternoon, just
like mechanics going to work.'

Luc Sante, *Low Life* (1991: 222)

The earliest film images of gangsters emerged in the 1900s as a result
of concerns over industrialisation and urbanisation in American life.
Turn-of -the-century Progressive reform movements often addressed
social problems caused by urban growth and social decay such as crime,
poverty, famine, and disease. Muckraking journalism and documentary
realism in photography helped expose the social conditions that led to
urban crime and criminality. Tabloid newspapers in the metropolises of
America also documented through illustrations and photography the
violent crimes associated with urban life, often exploiting violence itself
as a result. Though gangs had existed in the mid-nineteenth century and
were typically associated with Tammany Hall politics (referring to the graft

and political corruption associated with Boss Tweed and Tammany Hall in New York City) the gangster becomes an American cultural figure with the development of mass media culture in the twentieth century. Beginning with photographic documentary realism and early American cinema the gangster image develops in close relation to actual events that become increasingly well known in the media. According to Carlos Clarens, 'Crime films work in terms of transgression and retribution ... Because they are so near in time to actual events, crime films provide a useful means to review a major strain of American violence along a dynamic continuum' (1980: 14). In essence these films reflect the 'expression of America's changing attitudes toward crime' (ibid.). This 'dynamic continuum' can be documented through the shifting image of the film gangster from his origins in Progressive reform media through his development in the silent era into a cultural symbol for lawlessness and organised crime.

Before tracing this development it is necessary to distinguish the gangster film itself from the crime film. The crime film genre can encompass several sub-genres including the heist film, the murder mystery, *film noir*, the thriller, as well as the gangster film.[1] As a conceptual category the crime film is all encompassing and can denote several sub-categories, depending on their particular emphasis. The gangster film implies an emphasis on a central character or characters that are representative of organised criminal activity. Gangster film narratives, therefore, often highlight the life and actions of an organised crime figure either in personal power struggles or in conflict with representatives of law and order, fellow criminal associates, or rival gangs. The narrative focus in gangster films can either be on a central gangster protagonist or gangsterism itself as a threat to society. The gangster film often features an urban milieu that the gangster inhabits, as a space for transgression and illicit activity. Yet the genre, or sub-genre, is also distinguished by its generic flexibility in terms of thematic and historical variations based on its topicality. Typically based on source material from actual events derived primarily from print media such as newspapers, tabloids, and popular magazines, the gangster film can thus be viewed as a historical film that documents how urban crime was interpreted at particular junctures in American history. Through sensationalism and imaginative renderings of urban life, the image of the gangster increasingly becomes emblematic of the fear of modernity and technology particularly in its early cinematic manifestations.

Documenting Vice – Social Photographic Realism

Many scholarly works on the gangster film utilise the photography of Jacob Riis as a way to discuss the early cinematic representation of the American gangster during the Progressive era. As Jonathan Munby notes, 'taking their cue from the perspective established most powerfully in the photojournalism of Riis, in the teens and twenties gangster films represented gangsterdom as evidence of a degrading and evil modern world in need of "uplift"' (1999: 21). Likewise, Lee Grieveson contends that the visual culture of this period, including the work of Riis, 'was particularly important in delineating this dark and threatening space' (2005: 16) in urban centres through the mass press and sensationalised accounts of underworld life. Riis's photographs of New York slum tenements and tenement life along with his accompanying book, *How the Other Half Lives* (1890), brought attention to the social environment of the poor and destitute in an exposé fashion. His work is often linked with the muckraking journalism of the period and helped establish social documentary realism as a distinct style of photography. Considerably less known is the fact that Riis was a former police reporter for the *New York Tribune* and was familiar with the sensationalist tactics of newspaper journalism. Rather than observing the poor in the enclosed space of the crowded tenements, both Riis's urban street photographs and writings help establish a visual context for urban realism in the gangster film by creating a transgressive space.

In *How the Other Half Lives*, Riis discusses New York gangs and 'toughs' in his chapter titled, 'The Harvest of Tares'. Through the use of the metaphor of the garden as community, 'tares' refers to the weeds in the garden. Much like the popular journalism of the period, a cause-and-effect relationship is established with the social environment that produces the gang: 'The "growler" stood at the cradle of the tough. It bosses him through his boyhood apprenticeship in the "gang," and leaves him, for a time only, at the door of the jail that receives him to finish his training and turn him loose upon the world a thief' (Riis 2010: 124). For Riis the saloon, the jail, and the street are the urban environs that produce the gang, 'the ripe fruit of tenement-house growth' (2010: 125). The connection is thus made between physical environment, particularly those areas most often associated with transgression, and criminal behaviour. Riis goes on to describe the false bravado of the tough, his penchant for publicity (thereby explaining his willingness to be photographed) and the 'social clubs' where the gang meets, 'generally in a tenement, sometimes under a pier or a dump, to carouse, play cards, and plan their raids' (2010: 129). Much of their criminal activity consists of stealing and political ward activity, anything that pays them for their use of physical force and intimidation. This focus on the urban environment as a threatening and dangerous space is even more apparent in several Riis photographs that took advantage of actual locations and their inhabitants.

The Riis street photography emphasises a threatening space in the urban environment created by the structure of the tenements themselves. Rather than illicit empathy for the inhabitants of the tenements and their claustrophobic living conditions, these photographs of street life provided a more ominous viewpoint of the results of tenement life, particularly in regard to its younger inhabitants. The power of the photographs lay in the way that the viewer was able to share the space, as if they were in the room themselves. The attraction of the Riis street photographs were similar, but more in the sense of the viewer being able to practically rub elbows with criminality itself in a vicarious way. The viewer does not empathise with the subjects in these photographs but becomes either a transgressor or witness to their activity. One example of this viewer/subject relationship can be seen in the photograph titled, 'A Growler Gang in Session' (1890) (see Riis 2010: 131). The photograph depicts a group of seven young men seated in an outside location passing a growler of presumably beer amongst them. The subjects, all wearing hats, are seemingly caught off-guard by the photographer, rather than having posed for the picture. Though several are looking at the photographer, the remaining subjects are staring intently at the growler. The subjects, referred to as 'The Montgomery Guards', are quite possibly a juvenile street gang who are either celebrating a recent criminal victory or preparing for some type of criminal activity. Riis used the photograph as an illustration of 'toughs' in How the Other Half Lives, with a warning to the reader: 'Lest any reader be led into the error of supposing them to have been harmless fellows enjoying themselves in peace, let me say that within half an hour after our meeting, when I called at the police station three blocks away, I found there two of my friends the "Montgomery Guards" under arrest for robbing a Jewish pedlar [sic] ... and trying to saw his head off, as they put it, "just for fun"' (2010: 128). Riis's photographs of street gangs and his textual relation of their notorious activities subverts their seemingly harmless nature. The street photographs in particular are used by Riis to comment on the result of the crowded tenements of New York – the creation of the city tough, whose criminal gang activity undermine social order in the Progressive-era.

Perhaps the most famous photograph of this period, 'Bandits' Roost' (1888) emphasises a particular setting, rather than a criminal activity, as a transgressive place in the city.[2] The subject is an alleyway in the slums of New York where a motley group of inhabitants are pictured on either side of the narrow alley. Staring directly at the photographer, the subjects, predominately male, are framed in a threatening manner as though they have formed a gauntlet to provoke witnesses to enter. The natural light enters from the far end of the alley and reinforces this gauntlet-like atmos-

The urban spatial environment as threat at the turn of the century: Jacob Riis's 'Bandit's Roost' (1888)

phere by highlighting the viewer's perspective from darkness prevalent in the foreground and sides of the alley to the brightness of daylight in the background. The intimidating human subjects have no clear facial expressions and gaze vacant and unemotionally at the photographer. The photograph continues the 'mixture of fear and fascination' that is representative of Riis's depictions of slum life at the turn of the century and 'the slum dweller as threat' (Grieveson 2005: 23, 24). Gangster film scholars, to illustrate the city tough gangs that provided early gangster films with their subject matter, often use this particular photograph. Though this is no doubt true, its real importance to the gangster film lies in its depiction of the urban space as a malignant threat, an 'underworld' territorial space that ran counter to urban civility and social order. As Munby notes, 'we look not at the world as seen by the so-called bandits, but at a projection dictated by the middle-class perception of the slum-dweller as threat' (1999: 24). The setting of the crowded back alley, with its imposing human figures staring blankly into the camera, illustrates the influence of a claustrophobic environment on its inhabitants. An environment that produces the urban 'tough' as a figure of survival in the slums – and consequently a threat to moral order. This depiction of urban social realism showing the relationship between the physical and social environment and its inhabitants would become an integral characteristic of the gangster film.

Musketeers of Pig Alley (1912): D.W. Griffith's Depiction of the Gangster Evil

Often referred to as the first gangster film, D. W. Griffith's *Musketeers of Pig Alley* is important because it establishes certain visual and narrative conventions of the genre. Primarily through its semi-social documentary quality, the film provides a comparative dramatisation to the social realist photography of Jacob Riis. Accordingly, its milieu is populated with 'bars, alleys, dance halls, guns, cops, loyal sidekicks, and rival gangs' (Munby 1999: 24). Though there were earlier films depicting criminal gangs, such as *The Silver Wedding* (1906) and *The Black Hand* (1906), Griffith's film is instantly recognisable as a 'gangster film' due to the elements within it that would later become conventionalised.

The *Biograph Bulletin* entry for the film describes it as a 'depiction of the gangster evil' that was intended to show the public 'vividly the doings of the gangster type of people'. It then establishes a topical connection that will remain constant throughout the gangster genre. 'Much has been done, and is still being done, to wipe out this evil which has long been a menace to the respectable citizen and this picture shows the situation as it is, and the extreme necessity for radical action on the part of the authorities' (quoted in Usai 2002: 158). By referencing the topicality of the subject matter and its journalistic resource – 'Much is printed ... in the newspapers of the workings of the gangsters' (ibid.) – the advertising for the film creates a 'pulled from the headlines' approach that establishes a sense of authenticity. This social exposé approach was used to capitalise on the recent murder of Herman Rosenthal in New York City, often referenced as America's first gangland slaying. These recent events were even mentioned in the *Moving World* review of *Musketeers of Pig Alley* by claiming that the film was 'an underworld story which will remind many who see it of some recent happenings in New York City' (quoted in Usai 2002: 163). Primarily capitalising on the depiction of gangsters and gang life, Griffith's film offered the viewer an opportunity to vicariously observe the urban criminal experience.

The film opens with a title card that reads 'New York's Other Side', thereby referencing a spatial differentiation between two social environments: the haves and the have nots. Though the outdoor sequences of the film were actually shot in Fort Lee, New Jersey, both the title card and the lack of identifiable landmarks establish the setting as a realistic one to the viewer. Griffith keeps the individual shots tightly framed and alternates the tenement district spaces between interior locations (the tenement room, hallway, the dancehall all filmed at the Biograph Studio in New York) and exterior locations (the busy street, the alleyway). Griffith and his cameraman Billy Bitzer re-create the big-city atmosphere and claustrophobic spaces of the tenements through cramped interior settings and bustling crowds. The story itself concerns a young couple, the Little Lady and the Musician, who are destitute and in need of cash. The Snapper Kid, head of the Musketeers gang, encounters the Little Lady and during the Gangster's Ball saves her from being drugged by a rival gangster. The two rival gangs have a violent encounter in an alleyway, where the Musician is able to retrieve his stolen wallet. Fleeing the police, the Snapper Kid is aided by the Little Lady, who creates an alibi for him.

A unique aspect of the film are the outdoor scenes that closely resemble the social realist photography of Riis. As Munby suggests, Griffith

D. W. Griffith's 'depiction of the gangster evil' as a result of social environment:
Musketeers of Pig Alley (1912)

'attempted to extend Riis's perspective in his desire for a social realism
that would also feed the demand for reform (1999: 24). This is perhaps most
clear in the back alley scenes where the visual composition almost mirrors
that of Riis's photograph, 'Bandit's Roost'. In the first alley sequence, the
Musician encounters a friend and relates his good fortune in obtaining
money; all the while his conversation is overheard by the Snapper Kid and
his gangster crony (Harry Carey). The alleyway is overflowing with slum
dwellers and drunkards who seem to use it as a communal gathering place
to rid themselves of the crowded tenements. The setting parallels Riis's
photograph by showing only the outside walls of the tenement buildings
that frame the alleyway itself. A sense of depth creates a crowded spatial
environment as the only movement within the frame is vertical – much like
the gauntlet-like atmosphere in Riis's photograph. Other crowded social
spaces in the film include the dancehall where the Gangster's Ball takes
place, and the saloon attached to the dance hall where the rival gangster
attempts to drug the Little Lady. These spaces, as well as the alleyway,

represent the urban milieu of the gangster and his social sphere of influence. As such they will become transgressive spaces in the gangster film itself, urban spaces that breach the civil space with the uncivil, the world of law and order with vice and corruption. These urban areas of transgression (the dance club, the saloon/speakeasy, nightclub, the city street) will become a convention of the gangster genre even though they will change substantially over the years.

The film also helps to establish another narrative convention of the gangster film – the sympathetic gangster. Earlier crime films that centered on gang activity were shot primarily from a distance and focused on the crime itself (kidnapping, robbery). An important element in *Musketeers of Pig Alley* is that it has an identifiable gangster protagonist in the Snapper Kid. Elmer Booth's portrayal creates a likeable, cocky, impetuous, quick-tempered, city tough whose characterisation resembles what Robert Sklar refers to as the 'city boy' actors of the sound era: James Cagney, Humphrey Bogart, and John Garfield.[3] As Eugene Rosow asserts in his early history of the American gangster film,

> Like gangsters played by Cagney, the Snapper Kid is short, power-ful, explosive, and expressive with his body, face, and gestures. He is violent and quick to act in movements that snap out like his name. He is good-natured about the little lady's rejection, sly enough to avoid going to jail, wise enough not to fight in the Big Boss's place, and constantly putting plans into action to get what he wants. He exudes a healthy self-confidence and is proud of the snappy way he dresses. (1978: 70)

The characterisation of the sympathetic gangster would become a central development in the genre, as well as one of its most controversial aspects.

Another gangster convention that *Musketeers of Pig Alley* helped establish was that of civic corruption and graft. At the end of the film, Griffith shows the Snapper Kid accepting a bribe from an unknown person (a disembodied hand holding a wad of money is shown entering the frame and gesturing towards the Kid); the title card simply reads 'Links in the System'. Griffith expands on Lincoln Steffen's famous description of New York's criminal 'system' by showing the collusion of innocents, criminals, and the police within a protections-type racket ('I'll scratch your back if you scratch mine'). The title card implies that this system is 'normal' in an urban environment where the civil and uncivil intermingle with each other. According to Carlos Clarens, 'that disembodied hand was a ... metonymy for the whole corrupt, graft-ridden system' (1980: 19). Corruption and political graft would become a prominent motif throughout the history of the gangster genre, especially in films that concerned organised crime and the Syndicate. Although the *Musketeers of Pig Alley* established many of the generic conventions of the gangster film, another prominent film added social reform values in an attempt to showcase the efforts of Progressive movements in saving the criminal through redemption, as we shall now see.

Regeneration (1915): Gangster Redemption Narratives

Based on Owen Kildare's memoir *My Mamie Rose*, Raoul Walsh's debut film, *Regeneration*, often considered the first feature-length gangster film, is notable primarily because of its use of location photography and dramatic action sequences. Though the film is still very much grounded in the mixture of melodramatic elements within a social reform context, its depiction of the influence of environment and its underworld settings help establish the gangster's underworld milieu and location photography as key conventions of the genre. The shifting narrative space between domestic and underworld settings remains an important spatial relationship in the gangster film and originates in the early Progressive-era films, including (though to a lesser extent) *Musketeers of Pig Alley*. Drawing directly on the discourses about settlement houses and tenement life, the film makes social environment an important influence on criminal behaviours. As Lee Grieveson notes, the film is 'informed principally by a sense of the environmental causes of gang-related criminality ... counterpoised to the space of the tenement, saloon, and nightclub is the redemptive space of the settlement house' (2005: 29). Tenement life becomes a pattern of abuse, alcoholism, starvation, and deprivation and creates a need for survival of the fittest, or a vindication for violent behaviour. According to Carlos Clarens' assessment of the film, 'whereas Griffith exhibited a Victorian moral view of poverty and crime – the deserving criminal issuing from the deserving poor – Walsh elaborated his own brand of Social Darwinism: "the most

daring," "the quickest fist," assured the survival of the fittest in a competi-
tive society' (1980: 21).

The film relates the story of Owen Conway's (Rockliffe Fellowes) childhood development from an orphan who is taken in by abusive tenement
dwellers to his transformation into a gangster. Through his relationship
with a settlement house worker, Mary Deering (Anna Q. Nilsson), he is
reformed through her actions and death at the hands of one of his fellow
gangsters. The 'regeneration' of the title refers to the act of redemption
that is offered as a displacement to criminal behaviour. According to Fran
Mason, Owen's 'potential for "regeneration" is shown throughout the film
not only in a series of chivalric acts where he either rescues children or
saves underdog characters from a beating, but also in a scene in a music
hall where the image of him as a child eating an ice cream is transposed
over an image of him drinking a glass of beer"' (2002: 2), a visual indication of his loss of innocence. This regeneration is also present when he
decides not to seek vengeance for the death of Mary by killing his fellow
gangster, Skinny (William Sheer).

Often seen as a precursor to Walsh's later gangster films (*The Roaring
Twenties* (1939), *White Heat* (1949)), the film contains several action
sequences including a fire on an excursion barge, fights, and a climactic
escape sequence with the villainous gangster Skinny falling from a tenement clothesline. Walsh took full advantage of location photography in
the film using such New York City locations as the Chinatown district, the
Bowery, and the East Side tenements. The excursion barge sequence was
photographed on the Hudson River, near Nyack. This use of actual locations captured the city 'in teeming overhead panoramas that were more
expansive than Griffith's street-level shots' (Clarens 1980: 21). The emphasis on location photography extends the social realism that would become
integral to the gangster film. The street locations are juxtaposed with the
domestic sphere emphasising the dichotomy between the male space
of the street and the female-controlled environment of the settlement
house and the home. Walsh presents these spaces as different versions
of public and private spheres of influence. When Marie ventures out of
the settlement house she becomes vulnerable to criminal behaviour; and
when Owen ventures into the settlement house he becomes vulnerable
to societal reform and redemption. The melodramatic action sequences
throughout the film reflect the clash between these influences.

Progressive-era gangster films reflected the social reformist concerns with urban environmental influences on criminal behaviour. The growing development of cities magnified social problems related to poverty, crime, and corruption. Thus, one of the primary concerns of urban social reform was dealing with the criminal and the gang and their conversion to respectable and obedient citizens. Concurrently, early silent films often mirrored these problems within a melodramatic narrative structure coupled with social realist photography. These films often capitalised on the differentiation of the 'underworld' of vice and corruption and the 'civilised' world of culture and influence. Both *Musketeers of Pig Alley* and *Regeneration* contributed to the 'depiction of the gangster evil' by presenting sympathetic gangster protagonists whose criminal behaviour allowed viewers to vicariously indulge in the exciting urban experience of vice and violence. Though these early gangsters seem very distant to subsequent cinematic representations, they laid the foundation for the development of the anti-hero persona that would become central to the genre.

Underworld (1927) and The Racket (1928): The Birth of the Modern Gangster

The late 1920s ushered in a new image of the gangster as a social climber who was now part of the emerging urban middle-class. Characterised by capitalism, consumerism, and a corporate work ethic, the modern gangster became a symbol of the rampant consumption culture of the Jazz Age. No longer a social outcast, the gangster became a central figure in the negotiation of the new urbanism and modernity itself. As Munby asserts, 'the gangster film [of the 1920s] was a vehicle where the new consumer culture found its most exciting expression. The gangster was someone who had thrown off the straitjacket of bourgeois moral rectitude and had set about the business of selling pleasure' (1999: 24). Significantly this commodification of pleasure coincides with Prohibition and the enforcement of the Volstead Act, thereby, in many ways, making the consumption of pleasure a transgressive experience. The modern gangster was able to negotiate that urban experience for many through sartorial excess and extravagant consumption. Modernity in the form of the metropolis represented both a space for discipline and excess, where pleasure mixed with guilt and denial. The modern gangster cycle of the late 1920s showcased this metropolitan experience as well as the central iconic figure of that experience – the Gangster.

The depiction of the city in the modern gangster film cycle of the late 1920s exemplifies the 'Roaring Twenties' culture of a spendthrift modern consumer culture. The modern city becomes the central location in the gangster film and is no longer associated with the social realism of tene-ment life and the influence of environment but becomes the milieu that the gangster inhabits. The urban environment is no longer the real city (many of metropolitan settings in these films are now constructed in film studios) but are more indicative of Warshow's claim that the 'the real city … produces only criminals; the imaginary city produces the gangster' (1962: 131). Likewise, Fran Mason points out the importance of this setting and the licentiousness associated with it:

> The gangster movie is located in a city of the industrial and techno-logical, where traditional morality has become lax or non-existent, where the pleasure-principle and an easier enactment of sexuality and desire are possible (as represented by the night club and the speakeasy), where rationalization and routinization are dominant motifs (in the systematization of gang life into corporate struc-tures and the routinization of violence), and where commodities, consumerism and money form the desiring network in which the gangster locates himself. (2002: 15)

The industrial and technological aspects of city life are increasingly associ-ated with gangster culture and include automobiles, trucks, radios, tele-phones, as well as machine guns. The increased importance of modern technology in the gangster film allows the gangster to acquire *flâneur* status 'as a free-floating entity who lives his desires through the uncon-trolled movement around both the city and the culture of modernity' (ibid.). The modern gangster cycle of 1927/28, initiated by the success of Josef Von Sternberg's *Underworld* and further qualified by Lewis Milestone's *The Racket*,[4] showcased the modern metropolis and the gangster as *flâneur* and contributed to the development of the gangster as anti-hero in American cinema.

The carnivalesque urban metropolis of the Prohibition years becomes a significant convention of the modern gangster film and reflects the Jazz Age culture that it exemplifies. In contrast to the tenement-infested environs of Progressive-era crime films that fostered criminal activity, the modern gangster film is immersed into the neon-lighted, vertically expanded architecture of the modern city, where the gangster is in total control of urban space. Prohibition itself, not only serves as the gangster's *raison d'être* but provides the era with its Bakhtinian carnival aspect through its use of transgressive spaces for pleasure – the speakeasy and night club.[5] These spaces are also controlled by the gangster and allow his identification with licentious and profane pleasures. The modern gangster film that emerges in the late 1920s use these spaces in much more elaborate displays of the pleasures afforded to the viewer than in Progressive-era gangster films. By doing so they equate the gangster as a sympathetic character through his identification with the carnivalesque pleasure of transgression (the gangsters primary activity as bootlegger allows the public to covertly flaunt the law). The party sequences in *Underworld* and *The Racket* showcase the nightclub/speakeasy as a carnivalesque site of excess and misrule in the modern gangster film. These transgressive spaces inhabited by criminals and the public will become a convention of the Prohibition-era gangster and his mocking disdain for law-and-order. Likewise, they create a space for the gangster's empowerment through sartorial excess and prohibited pleasure.

The 'Devil's carnival party' sequence in Von Sternberg's *Underworld* showcases the gangster's consumption-oriented milieu through its mise-en-scène and narrative action. Similar to the Gangster's Ball sequence in Griffith's film, it is much more carnivalesque in appearance. Paper party streamers abound on the ceiling and floor of the large ballroom where the gangsters are celebrating the 'underworld's annual armistice'. Adding to the carnival atmosphere is a large statue of a crowned bull steer – not only a symbol of the misrule of the film's gangster protagonist, 'Bull' Weed (George Bancroft) but also a symbol of sexual power and potency. The sequence celebrates the licentiousness of gangsterism through its focus on prankster-like activities and excessive behaviour (primarily drunkenness). The gangsters themselves look out of place dressed in formal attire, their physical bodies constrained in the tight fitting clothes they wear to try and look 'respectable'. The ballroom is crowded and equally constrained, populated as it is with the bodies of the numerous revelers. At one point in the sequence there is a brief montage of the faces of the revelers who look even more grotesque in appearance. Practical jokes abound, primarily through the character of 'Slippy' Lewis (played by silent

A symbolic centerpiece display of 'Bull' Weed's consumptive power and sexual potency:
Underworld (1927)

film comedian Larry Semon) who brandishes and shoots a water pistol at a fellow hoodlum and spits metal 'bb's' at Bull Weed's neck. The consumption culture of the 'Roaring Twenties' is best exemplified by the highlight of the festivities – the crowning of the 'Queen of the Ball'. A large tally board is used to keep track of the votes throughout the evening, as if it were exchanges of commodities in the stock market. At party's end, Bull Weed's 'girl', 'Feathers', is to be crowned 'Queen' – an effective symbol of the commodity-oriented culture of the Prohibition gangster. The 'armistice' nature of the proceedings, however, end in violence – with the attempted rape of 'Feathers' by rival gangster, 'Buck' (another symbol of animalistic sexual potency) Mulligan (Fred Kohler) and the subsequent shooting of Mulligan by Bull Weed. The carnivalesque nature of the party sequence becomes a metonym for the exuberant lifestyle and excessive behavior of the modern gangster.

Similarly, Milestone's *The Racket* contains a party sequence that focuses on the carnivalesque as a space for misrule and rampant consumerism. Gangster Nick Scarsi (Louis Wolheim) provides a birthday celebra-tion for his younger brother, Joe (George E. Stone) at a speakeasy that is hidden inside a conventional and sparsely populated café. Among the invited guests is Scarsi's nemesis, Captain McQuigg (Thomas Meighan), a police officer intent on arresting him any chance he gets. In an example of the topsy-turvy carnivalesque revelry of the gangster's milieu, Scarsi has outmaneuvered McQuigg by having his henchman released (by writ of *habeas corpus* – the gangster's preferred legal tool) from a murder rap. As the henchman shows up to take his assigned place at the party table occupied by the police captain, McQuigg says, 'All right, Nick – that's a horse on me', referring to Scarsi's gamesmanship in foiling his plans once again. The sequence, similar to the 'Devil's carnival' is filled with revelers, dancers, and jazz musicians. During the sequence a rival gangster, Spike Corcoran (Henry Sedley), enters with his mob intent on confronting Nick, who has commandeered a shipment of booze. Sitting opposite one another from across the room, they stare intently at each other, until a shot is fired and Corcoran stiffly falls across his table revealing a revolver in his hand hidden beneath a napkin. Nick, suspecting an assassination attempt, has sized the matter up and shot first, knowing that Corcoran was about to do the same. The carnival-like atmosphere of the speakeasy has ended, like that in *Underworld,* with violent action. Throughout the sequence, as well as the film, Nick Scarsi is characterized by his boisterous laughter, as if he were deliberately mocking societal convention and normative behaviour. Both Bull Weed and Nick Scarsi are indicative of the modern gangster as *flâneur* in that they represent 'the unlimited and excessive modes of action and desire-fulfillment that modernity allows' (Mason 2002: 15). Both gang-ster protagonists actively control the spatial environment of the modern city and transgress the physical boundaries of class and society through the commodity of illicit pleasure.

The modern gangster cycle of the late 1920s centres on the gangster and his world and the film narratives within this cycle primarily focus on the criminal perspective. This is particularly important in the development of the genre because it establishes the romanticised notion of the anti-hero who 'becomes archetypal because he refuses to bow down to the systems of law and ideology which ultimately destroys him' (Mason 2002: 7). No longer the outcast figure of the tenements, the gangster is now an insider who is able to function in modernity through its technological innovations.

Both Bull Weed in *Underworld* and Nick Scarsi in *The Racket* represent the modern gangster as protagonist in films that showcase the gangster as anti-hero who flaunts law and order in his attempt at self-gratification and desire. It is significant that Chicago journalists Ben Hecht and Bartlett Cormack, who inscribed the larger-than-life characterisations with personality and heroic status, wrote both films. Bull Weed sacrifices himself for a personal cause at the end of Sternberg's film, while Nick Scarsi dies while attempting to escape, the victim of the corrupt system that pervades Milestone's. These films establish the template for the modern gangster who would become even more pronounced and threatening to moral guardians with the introduction of sound.

Notes

1 For further discussion of the crime film see Leitch (2002) and Thompson (2007).
2 This photograph in particular is typically the central focus for gangster film scholars in discussions of D. W. Griffith's *Musketeers of Pig Alley*; see Rosow (1978), Munby (1999) and Usai (2002).
3 See Sklar (1992); he categorises the 'city boy' as a cultural type and examines the film careers and screen roles of three metropolitan actors (Cagney, Bogart, and Garfield) as focal points for the cultural shift from agrarian values to urban ones.
4 Milestone's *The Racket* presents an interesting historiographic study in that until relatively recently it was considered a 'lost film'. After the death of Howard Hughes in 1976 a 35mm print was found among his artifacts and the film was restored by the University of Nevada, Las Vegas. Though not available as yet on DVD, it has been frequently broadcast on the Turner Classic Movies cable channel. Most of the standard histories of the gangster film may mention the film, but rarely go into details or analysis, simply because it was unavailable for study. This is perhaps one reason that Von Sternberg's *Underworld* has received so much attention by scholars and critics.
5 The reference to Mikhail Bakhtin is significant, especially to the Prohibition-era gangster films. Prohibition itself becomes a carnival where societal laws are ignored and illegality, in the form of bootlegging and rum running, are representative of forbidden pleasures. Bahktin's

use of aspects of the carnivalesque such as billingsgate (coarse language), banquet imagery, and the grotesque are clearly relevant to the gangster and his social function in the carnival of Prohibition America during the 1920s and early 1930s.

2 THE RACKETEER AND THE OUTLAW:
GANGSTER ARCHETYPES OF THE 1930S

> For hardly a day passes in any large city that some youth – arrested
> for murder, robbery or other violent crime – does not declare to the
> police that he 'did it' because he wanted to be like those glam-
> orous characters he read about in the newspapers. The gangster,
> gunman, racketeer, and rum runner (as pictured by the press) are
> to many young men what Young Wild West and Deadwood Dick
> were to thousands of youths a generation ago.
>
> Morrow Mayo, 'Glorifying the Criminal' (1931: 438)

The excerpt above from the *Commonweal* admonished the American
press, particularly tabloid newspapers such as the *Daily Mirror* and the
Daily News, for sensationalising crime reporting during the early 1930s
and serving as a 'barker for crime and a press agent for criminals' (ibid.).
The author further claimed that the part crime played in the daily press
was 'out of all proportion to its news value' (1931: 438) and was simply
created for sensational effect. Although it centres on journalism, its indict-
ment of the glorification of the criminal is, and was, extended to include
the motion picture. Nearly one hundred gangster pictures were produced
between 1930 and 1932, including the 'classic' trio of films, *Little Caesar*
(1930), *The Public Enemy* (1931), and *Scarface* (1932). The article references
earlier criminal models from the dime novels of the nineteenth century as

fomenting a similar admiration among American youth. But a distinction should be made between the frontier bandit and the gangster/racketeer comparison that the author makes. In the 1930s this distinction between the racketeer and the outlaw created two gangster archetypes that remain conceptual models for the American gangster film.

Both Al Capone and John Dillinger served as real-life models for the conceptualisation of the racketeer and the outlaw in the press and in film. The tabloids and popular magazines, particularly the pulps, promoted these figures as models for racketeering and banditry in the 1930s. In the mid-1930s a cultural shift occurred in the representation of gangster imagery that was caused by several historical events: the end of Prohibition, the crime wave of 1933/34, and the enforcement of the Hollywood Production Code. These events marked a fragmentation of the gangster into two basic archetypes that would be further fragmented by generic variations in the late 1930s due to concerns of moral guardians over the gangster film that originated in the early part of the decade. Much of these concerns were actually instigated by the effects of the nascent sound technology on the genre. As Fran Mason asserts,

> The gangster's transgressive and excessive elements are more immediately evoked in the sound era and he comes to be an embodiment of the threat of the modern, not only in the literal threat of the violence of the gun, but in his mobility, which challenged the established hierarchies that the ideological messages of the sound gangster film often tried to defend. (2002: 4)

This mobility is evident in the way sound exacerbated the image of the gangster through his vernacular and ethnic language, his social status, his adoption of modern business methods, and his abrasive assertiveness. By contrast the outlaw is notable for exemplifying the final vestiges of American individualism and the frontier spirit, as well as the social concerns of Depression-era America. The outlaw was able to survive the Hays Office because of the federal law-and-order meta-narrative that became associated with the image, whereas the racketeer image was subsumed into other film genres until the post-war period.

Warner Bros. was the Hollywood studio that contributed significantly to the depiction of these two archetypes during the 1930s. The gangster film was part of the Warner Bros. overall economic survival strategy in the early 1930s of producing inexpensive and quickly made topical films with urban subjects and settings. This also created a need for a stable of new stars that were street smart, urban types prolific in the street-wise vernacular such as James Cagney, Edward G. Robinson, Joan Blondell, Lee Tracy, and Humphrey Bogart. The Warner Bros. films also developed a distinct economic fast-paced style that emulated the urban setting itself. Briskly-paced, these films rarely exceed eighty minutes and are noted for their quick edits and montage sequences. In this sense they are analogous to the tabloid journalistic style that frequently provided their source material. This tabloid narrative style created a populist audience familiar with the subject matter and events as well as the hard-boiled writing of contemporary newspapers and pulp fiction. As Nick Roddick notes, the Warner Bros. gangster cycle 'responded to and reflected contemporary concerns' (1983: 99) and were immensely popular in the process. This popularity drew the attention of state and local censorship offices, as well as moral guardians concerned with not only the content, but also the action-driven style and its implications for American values.

In this chapter, we will examine the cultural and industrial development of the racketeer and the outlaw in American gangster cinema during the 1930s. Both archetypes originated in historical circumstances that were 'contemporary concerns' for their audiences, namely Prohibition and the Depression. In hindsight, today's audiences when viewing films such as *Little Caesar* or *Scarface* are not as aware of their historical reception as topical films and the issues raised within them. These issues and the central characters in the films created a discourse on motion picture content that impacted the development of the gangster film during the Hollywood studio era. According to Mason, the issues raised by the gangster film reveal 'the contradictions of the existing social order even while it mapped its ideology' (2002: 30). But censorial efforts to confine and control gangster imagery only allowed for variations on a theme that illustrated his cultural significance in American film.

Sound Technology and the Gangster Film

Although the importance of sound to the gangster genre cannot be overemphasised, it is the cultural impact of the technology on gangster imagery that is particularly significant in regards to its historical context. Film sound in the gangster film created an aural spatial environment that highlighted the problems of modernity and the urban environment. This aural component to the gangster also often emphasised both his social class and ethnicity, thereby creating a moral panic in the 1930s that was assuaged by the eventual moratorium on gangster films in 1935. According to Jonathan Munby,

> The gangster's tough vernacular voice only enhanced his status as an outspoken representative of the *vox populi*. The growing change in the perception of these once 'othered,' 'ghettoized,' and 'unnatural' Americans was accelerated by a cinematic culture now wired for sound, one disposed, finally to listen to formerly silent voices. (1999: 43)

This aural component becomes central to the gangster's control of environment through language and his negotiation of space through vernacular. This vernacular voice is also associated with the metropolitan performance style of many actors who become associated with the genre during the 1930s. The popularity of the gangster film genre in the early 1930s can be attributed to the way sound technology influenced not only performance style but also the streamlined visual style of the gangster film. Both spoken dialogue and sound effects created an expressivity that was hitherto not possible with silent film. No longer dependent on inter-titles to communicate exposition and additional narrative information, sound allowed for more fluid narrative development (at least after the experimental film sound period).

In the late 1920s sound technology created an experimental transitional period in Hollywood film production that affected the gangster film through its emphasis on dialogue. Although the films of this period seem visually awkward and overly enunciated when viewed today, their primary attraction for audiences, at least for a while, was the colorful argot of the gangster characters. By 1931, the sound technology and sound editing practices had become assimilated by the studios paving the way for the 'classic' films to emerge. Warner Bros.' *Lights of New York* (1928), the first all-talking picture, provided the template for the early sound gangster films of 1929, such as *Broadway, Weary River, Alibi,* and *Voice of the City.* The emphasis throughout these films is specifically on dialogue rather than dramatic action. As Carlos Clarens notes, many of these transitional sound gangster films 'came to rely on the most banal dialogue while all violence was consummated off-screen' (1980: 44). Yet these films were popular with audiences *because* of the novelty of sound. It is important to note that the gangster films in this early sound talking cycle stressed the gangster argot as a sound selling device; thereby creating an awareness of gangster 'speak' as an attraction for consumers. But when the argot delivery became noticeably over-done and carefully enunciated, its status as attraction was considered theatrical rather than real. Eventually oversaturation occurred and audiences became increasingly aware of 'aural overstimulation' by associating too much talking with excess theatricality (see Crafton 1997: 353–4). This provided the impetus for more realistic vernacular voices in the gangster cycle that emerged in the 1930–31 period when recorded sound dialogue became less theatrical in delivery and more realistic – perhaps too realistic.

The gangster film's use of vernacular was influenced by the writing style of hard-boiled fiction and newspaper journalism during the 1920s. The terse, forceful vernacular style of writers such as Dashiell Hammett, W.R. Burnett, and Ben Hecht among others was a masculine, aggressive style of writing that appealed to primarily working-class readers. Joseph Thompson Shaw, the editor of *Black Mask* magazine, once described its ideal readers as, 'vigorous-minded, hard ... responsive to the thrill of danger, the stirring exhilaration of clean, swift, hard action ... who know the song of the bullet. The soft, slithering hiss of a swift-thrown knife, the feel of hard fists, the call of courage' (quoted in Smith 2000: 28). As Shaw's prose style attests, the description is void of complexity as well as verbosity – and is representative of the short, direct prose contained in his magazine. Hard-boiled dialogue also reflected its male working-class readership through its use of urban vernacular and underworld slang that would likewise dominate the language in gangster films. One example can be found in the writing of Frederick Nebel whose novel *Crimes of Richmond City* was published in serialised form in *Black Mask* from September 1928 through May 1929. The dialogue exchange between Police Captain Steve MacBride and news reporter Kennedy showcases the hard-boiled style emphasis on vernacular:

'Something's got to break, Mac. When a bootlegging grease-
ball starts to run a town, starts to run the Department, something's got to break.'

'He's not running *me!*' barked MacBride.

'The hell he isn't! Don't tell me. I'm no greenhorn, Mac. Maybe
not you, personally. But your hands are tied. He's running somebody else, and somebody else is running somebody else, and the
last somebody else is running you.'

'You're talking through your hat, Kennedy.'

(Penzler 2007: 658)

This style is not only easily understood (especially by an often marginalised readership) but is emblematic of hard-boiled fiction in its short-
sentence length, word length, and word familiarity (especially its use of
contemporaneous slang expressions). This created a proletarian prose
style that reflected its primarily working-class male readership. When
this use of the vernacular voice is made audible in gangster films of the
1930s it creates what Sarah Kozloff refers to as 'anti-language' that the
gangster embraces as a means of aggressively controlling his environment
(2000: 202). This anti-language is marked by the profuse use of slang
and a specialised vocabulary, with words and phrases such as 'bulls',
'contract', 'a good egg', 'Baumes rush', 'bracelets', 'cabbage', and 'moll'
among others. As Kozloff suggests, this specialised vocabulary creates a
'symbolic boundary between a single group and the rest of society' (2000:
201) that also represents a power structure dynamic. One example of this
language dynamic, which bears comparison to the hard-boiled example
above, is from *Little Caesar* when, following an assassination attempt by a
rival gang, Rico Bandello (Edward G. Robinson) takes control of Little Arnie
Lorch's (Maurice Black) territory:

Rico: Arnie, you oughta had better sense than to hire a couple of
        outside yaps! Especially bad shots. You hired these mugs, they
        missed. Now you're through. If you ain't out of town by tomor-
        row mornin', you won't never leave it except in a pine box!
(Arnie, completely unnerved, actually trembling, doesn't reply)
Rico: I'm takin' over this territory ... from now on, it's mine. ...
        Better quit the racket, Arnie. You got so you can dish it out,

Rico Bandello and the articulation of power through 'anti-language': *Little Caesar* (1931)

but you can't take it no more. And you can take your hats and
beat it. The first thing you know you'll be arrested for firing a
rod in the city limits. Well, I guess that's about all. Pleasant
trip, gents. *(To his men)* Come on, boys.

Rico's banter is intimidating and forceful, making its points succinctly and
effectively. But what is most significant is that the language is the focus of
power, for most of the sequence Rico remains sitting in a chair with his feet
on a desk. The colorful argot of the underworld creates an alternative language structure to the norm, a language structure that places an emphasis
on the subversion of language as means of transgression. The audibility of
gangster dialogue, therefore, highlighted his transgressive nature as well
as his lower-class origins and ethnicity.

Similarly, Jonathan Munby addresses the importance of sound in
the early gangster film through its dialogic aspect that emphasised the
gangster's 'otherness'. According to Munby, the gangster spoke a 'street
vernacular in the accents of groups designated as cultural "others"' (1999:

39). The more realistic use of sound in the early 1930s was able to estab-lish a less theatrically enunciatory vocal style of delivery that incorporated more common, street-wise, realistic vocal stylisation. The actors associ-ated with this style were also associated with popular and ethnic theatri-cal traditions: Edward G. Robinson, James Cagney, and Paul Muni. Their gangster characterisations effectively represented a 'collusion of real and cinematic identity' (1999: 63) that was compounded by their vernacular voices. As Munby asserts the biographical proximity of these actors to their criminal personas, 'helped these gangsters speak less as characters in someone else's story than as authors of their own tales' (ibid.). Likewise, Robert Sklar acknowledges the emergence during the early sound period of the twentieth-century mass media phenomenon known as City Boys. The city boy is a performance type 'rooted in the language and manner-isms of urban male street life' (1992: xii). Sklar's study focuses on three performers who he associates with the city boy persona: James Cagney, Humphrey Bogart, and John Garfield – though he admits that there are a host of others (as well as city girl types such as Joan Blondell, Glenda Farrell, and Ann Dvorak). Sklar notes that the emergence of this cultural image coincides with and is popularised by the advent of both the talking picture and the Great Depression. The popular reception of the city boy and gangster image is related to his vernacular voice and its cultural sig-nificance. This remains an important element to the gangster film and the performance style associated with it. Vernacular voices from James Cagney to Steve Buscemi and characters from Tony Camonte to Tony Soprano sanc-tion the gangster's desire to subvert society through language. Gangster 'speak' is a means of control for the mobster whose vocal performance style often denotes his cultural heritage and social status. The gangster's broken grammar and awkward syntax were important components for cre-ating his subversion of social order that was representative of a primarily WASP culture that categorised him as 'other'. The anti-language of the underworld becomes as powerful a weapon for the cinematic gangster as the Tommy gun.

Prohibition and the Racketeer

In the episode of the science fiction television series *Star Trek* (NBC, 1966–69) titled, 'A Piece of the Action', Captain Kirk and Mr. Spock make contact with the inhabitants of planet Sigma Iotia II, in order to investigate the disappearance of a Federation ship a hundred years earlier. When they beam down to the planet what they encounter leaves them both astonished and curious. The Sigma Iotians have created a culture based on the Prohibition-era gangsters of Chicago. It is discovered that the missing Federation ship left behind a book titled, *Chicago Mobs of the Twenties*. Roaring Twenties America has been replicated by the Iotians down to the automobiles, clothes, and Thompson machine guns. Similar to 1920s Chicago mob culture the planet is divided into gangland factions vying for dominance. Kirk and Spock first encounter gang boss, Oxmyx (Anthony Caruso) who is interested in acquiring some of their phasers, referring to them in gangland parlance as 'heaters'. Kirk and Spock are kidnapped by rival gangster Jojo Krako (Vic Tayback) who wants 'to take over the territory' with the same 'heaters'. Eventually Kirk convinces the warring factions to form a single operation, a syndicate, with the Federation receiving a cut of their take. The episode ends with Kirk and Spock becoming aware that a communicator was inadvertently left behind in Oxmyx's office. Kirk fears that the time may come when the Iotians will demand a 'piece of *our* action'. The episode, first broadcast in 1968, continually plays on the iconography and vernacular language associated with the American gangster image of the racketeer. This image often becomes the stereotypical one when the conceptual idea of the 'American gangster' is mentioned, and is often caricatured (as in the *Star Trek* episode) in popular culture.

The cultural image of the racketeer dominates the early sound films of the 1930s because of its topicality to the entrepreneurial activity of bootlegging during the Prohibition era (1919–33). Prohibition created an opportunity for organised lawlessness in the form of bootlegging, rum running, and racketeering. The racketeer invokes a populist rebellious spirit who is essentially providing a service to the public and by doing so flaunting an unpopular law. In turn this led to a trend towards crime as a business enterprise involving modernised business methods and practices, and becomes a major component of the racketeer image of the gangster in American culture. Calvin Coolidge's remark that 'the business of America is business' became the motto for organised crime in the 1920s when gangsters shifted their locus of activity from the ethnic ghettoes to downtown business districts and adopted modern business strategies such as growth, consolidation, and organisation. No longer associated with street crime and armed robbery, the racketeer focused on providing goods (albeit illegal goods) to a thirsty consumer base and adopted middle-class business practices in order to better market and sell his product. This cultural shift, with its accompanying sartorial excess, became more and more apparent in the late 1920s when Hollywood films 'began to depict gangsters as nattily dressed, office-using businessmen. Pleasant-featured, they wore three-piece suits, ties, hats, and watch-chains – a stylish version of standard middle-class business attire' (Ruth 1996: 41). The historical paradigm for this cultural image was its most advertised and colorful proponent – Al Capone.

As David Ruth claims, the Capone legend was created, fostered, and chronicled by newspaper journalists and popular writers such as Ben Hecht, Fred D. Pasley, Walter Noble Burns, Richard T. Enright and others. Books such as *Al Capone: The Biography of a Self-Made Man* (1930), applied a Horatio Alger template to the Capone image by creating an individual success narrative in terms of business models. This 'cultural invention' helped 'personalize the generic gangster by giving him a particular name, city, and career' (Ruth 1996: 118) and in the process created a paradigm for the racketeer as modern businessman. Alphonse Capone (1899–1947) has become, through their efforts, as well as the films that were patterned from his persona and career, the dominant image of the Prohibition-era gangster in American culture.[1] In 1931 Capone made the claim that his activities were legitimate business practices: 'I'm just a businessman ... my rackets are run along strict American lines. This American system of ours – call it capitalism, call it what you like – gives each and every one of us a great opportunity, if we only seize it with both hands and make the most of it ... I've made my money by supplying a popular demand' (quoted in Maltby 2001: 127). It is the entrepreneurial aspect of the Capone legend that is central to the construction of the racketeer image.

Capone's personal philosophy concerning racketeering as business enterprise reveals several central themes prevalent in the racketeer archetype. The first of these is, similar to the Horatio Alger myth, the 'individual's escape from obscurity to wealth, power, and fame' (Ruth 1996: 123). If you do not seize opportunity 'with both hands', as Capone suggests, it will pass you by. Coincidentally, this 'rise-to-success from the lower ranks of criminality' theme is one of the gangster genre's most popular story lines and is found in the three classic gangster films of the early 1930s:

Little Caesar, *The Public Enemy*, and *Scarface*. Directly related to this is the idea that 'aggressive masculinity and modern business organization could co-exist' (Ruth 1996: 128). This aggressive masculinity is often displayed by overt physicality and violence, as well as assertive language. This becomes a dominant theme of the racketeer and is often reiterated in films from *Scarface* to *Murder, Inc.* (1960). The racketeer often dispenses sound organisational business practices through his desire to organise and eliminate cutthroat competition. The idea of the self-sufficient man is another theme that was also prevalent in the 1920s. Individuals such as Henry Ford and Charles Lindbergh created successful personas because of their accomplishments and acts of individual will and creativity.

The final theme that distinguishes the racketeer is that 'consumption could bring remarkable individual transformation' (Ruth 1996: 136). The racketeer becomes a hyperbolic metaphor for the consumer-driven, hedonistic Jazz Age. According to David Ruth, 'Capone's rise confirmed that modern commercial society awarded to the worthy the chance to remake themselves. Any person, even from the lowest stratum, had the opportunity to earn the purchasable pleasures that marked success in modern society' (1996: 136). This style of consumption is outwardly evident in the racketeer's appearance: his clothes, jewellry, automobiles, and leisure luxury items. The racketeer is distinguished by his accumulation of wealth, which is displayed through his consumption. But this excessive consumer activity and style was a façade that attempted to hide the gangster's ethnic origins and class status. Ruth further claims that the media creators of 'the gangster often suggested that the new criteria of stylish consumption threatened to undermine older categories of social classification' (1996: 71). This ultimately led to the moral panic and eventual censorship of gangster films in the 1930s.

Ultimately, there are several reasons that the Capone paradigm of the racketeer became culturally significant. It is emblematic of the Jazz Age cultural emphasis on stylish consumption. It reflects the cultural shift of the gangster image from the street hood's 'survival of the fittest' criminality into organised crime that is established along modern centralised business methods. It focuses on aggressive masculinity as an indication of individual success as well as business acumen. And it establishes a nostalgic memory of the Prohibition-era as a 'lawless decade' where criminal entrepreneurial efforts flourished as a part of American society. The bootlegger, the speakeasy, hip flasks, and bathtub gin were lexical indicators of a transgressive culture that existed in the 1920s and early 1930s. This sub-culture flaunted the law and participated in a Bakhtin-like carnivalesque period in American history when the consumption of alcohol was made illegal. It was a period that was documented and made famous as a means of economic survival by its most noted Hollywood chronicler – Warner Bros.

Warner Bros. and the Classic Gangster Production Cycle

The Warner Bros. gangster films of the early 1930s that helped establish the narrative and stylistic conventions of the genre are best understood in regard to the economic imperative of the studio during the initial years of the Depression. During the 1920s Warner Bros. financial investment in sound technology eventually began to pay-off with the box-office success of early sound feature films such as *Don Juan* (1927), *The Jazz Singer* (1927) and the all-talking picture, *Lights of New York* (1928). But the studio became 'particularly vulnerable when the depression hit' and as earnings plummeted, production costs were cut back. As part of this cost-cutting strategy more modestly budgeted films were put into production (see Glancy 1995: 60).[2] It was during this period that Darryl F. Zanuck became Warner Bros.' head of production (1930–33) and instigated the economic production shift to 'headline' films.

Zanuck once described the attributes of the 'headline' film as having 'the punch and smash that would entitle it to be a headline on the front page of any successful metropolitan daily' (quoted in Behlmer 1985: 9). This identifies two tabloid characteristics of the headline or topical film that became the bread-and-butter product of Warner Bros. in the early 1930s: contemporary in content and exposé-oriented. The headline film was not strictly speaking either a genre or a cycle but rather an 'operational approach' that exploited a current 'big news' event. According to Penelope Pelizzon and Nancy West, the headline film often referenced news items that were 'sensational enough to have received substantial press time' (2010: 55). This tabloid style was not uncommon to Zanuck, who began his career at Warner Bros. as a proficient scriptwriter in 1923 and had also written for pulp magazines. Sensational 'big news' events often centered on crimes such as the St. Valentine's Day Massacre and the Lindbergh kidnapping. Warner Bros.' headline films were economical

because of the contemporaneous settings and their use of contract play-
ers. These films were also made in different genres such as the newspaper
film (*Five Star Final*, 1931), the shyster lawyer film (*The Mouthpiece*, 1932),
the fallen woman film (*Baby Face*, 1931) and the racing film (*The Crowd
Roars*, 1932) as well as the gangster film. According to Nick Roddick, the
'headline films' were 'rarely prestige productions but could be counted
on to do solid business in the small-town and neighborhood theatres,
regularly giving a large return for a comparatively small investment' (1983:
99). Warner Bros.' *Doorway to Hell* (1930) is important because it not only
initiated the gangster cycle of the early 1930s but also exemplified some of
the basic features that would be re-fashioned to popularise the genre with
Depression-era audiences.

   Because of the close proximity in production dates the Warner Bros.
gangster films of 1930/31 can be seen as a part of the 'headline pictures'
strategy and as a production cycle of gangster films. Initiated by the
October 1930 release of *Doorway to Hell* and the unprecedented box-office
success of *Little Caesar* in January 1931 followed by the release of *The Public
Enemy* in May 1931, the cycle established the image of the racketeer with
Depression-era audiences. As mentioned earlier, this image is modelled
on Al Capone who was prominent in newspapers since the St. Valentine's
Day Massacre in 1929 and being named 'Public Enemy #1' by the Chicago
Crime Commission on 23 April 1930. During the summer of 1931, Capone
was indicted on several counts of federal tax evasion with his forthcoming
trial set for October. So concurrent with Warner Bros.' gangster cycle, the
tabloid crime news of America's most notorious racketeer was very much
a part of the topical landscape. Many film reviews noted the similarities
among characters and events displayed on screen. This cultural parallel
between history and film contributed to the development of the racketeer
image in gangster films. J.E. Smyth notes that these films 'witnessed a new
engagement with contemporary history and the boundary between journalism and history' (2010: 539). The cultural image of the racketeer could only
arise out of the Depression because it establishes a survival and success
mythos as well as a critique of Prohibition that appealed to contemporary
audiences. Whereas many of the films of this period are often viewed as
escapist and non-topical entertainments created to take the minds of the
audiences off the outside world, the gangster film was designed to 'reflect
the discontent and alienation, the deep anxiety and hostility, of many

Americans facing the Depression' (Peary 1981: 11). Its most prominent spokesperson and model for criminal success was the racketeer – a cultural image that valued success above all things, a critique of the American Dream at a time when it had become the American Nightmare.

The racketeer protagonist is the main characteristic of the gangster films of the early 1930s. It is a feature not only of the Warner Bros. cycle but also of other contemporaneous gangster films such as *Born Reckless* (Fox, 1930), *City Streets* (Paramount, 1931), *Gentleman's Fate* (MGM, 1931) and *Quick Millions* (Fox, 1931). The paradigm of the racketeer in these films addresses issues concerning class, ethnicity, and business strategy that marked the cultural shift in the gangster image that occurred in the late 1920s. These films are often marked by either a clear rise-and-fall narrative structure or a decline-and-fall structure charting the 'fall from grace' of the gangster protagonist. The importance here is that the gangster is the central narrative focus and is typically portrayed by the star actor, thereby creating sympathy toward the character. As mentioned earlier in this chapter, this sympathy becomes exacerbated by the use of sound, particularly through dialogue, but also through sound effects. These films depict a subversive vision of Depression-era America where survival is based on criminal success in industries such as bootlegging and racketeering. The racketeer becomes a populist hero during the Depression because of his ability to achieve his goals through physical force and persuasive powerful language. The racketeer is also of the people because of his naturalistic demeanour and street-wise vernacular with its specialised vocabulary. Yet in all the classic gangster films, the racketeer is doomed by his success and though he may reach the 'top of the world', he shortly meets his precipitous end. What became especially troubling for the moral guardians of the era was the glamourisation of the gangster and the characterisation of the racketeer in the mass media.

Archie Mayo's *Doorway to Hell* focuses entirely on the racketeer, Louie Ricarno (Lew Ayres) and his efforts to organise and maintain his criminal business association. Ricarno is already in charge at the beginning of the film and consolidates his criminal organisation in a scene where he forces other gang leaders to form a syndicate for their own benefit. 'We're in a big business. The only thing wrong with it is that it needs organizing and it needs a boss. I'm taking over both jobs', Ricarno politely informs the gang leaders he has gathered together for a meeting. Ricarno's concept of self-importance is also indicated at the end of the film when he is holed up in a one-room apartment fleeing from the police and fellow gangsters; prominently displayed on the apartment wall is a picture of 'Napoleon in Exile'. The idolisation of Napoleon occurs in several gangster films from this period and indicates not only an inflated ego but also a recognisable metaphor for the rise-and-fall narrative structures in many of the films. The characterisation of Ricarno is based on a composite of several historical gangsters, primarily Johnny Torrio and Al Capone. Like Torrio, Ricarno leaves the rackets, and similar to Capone he retires to an estate in Florida. The St. Valentine's Day Massacre is even indirectly addressed in the film through a newspaper spread showing photos from a gangland-style killing. The *New York Times* critic, Mordaunt Hall noting the relationship of the film to current headlines said that it 'will bring the flavor of familiar things to a public that has watched with growing alarm the reckless activities of gangland' (1930: 23). Ricarno is meticulously dressed with homburg, carnation in his lapel, and kid gloves. His demeanour is that of a middle-class businessman who is articulate enough to want to write his own memoirs – which he does, thereby providing the film with its rise-and-fall narrative structure. Ricarno even plays golf at his country estate, a true indication of his middle-class leisure position as a former racketeer. Ricarno's demeanour, however, belies his true status – he is perhaps too articulate. His speech is void of the colourful argot that we associate with the gangster. The vernacular gangster speak is primarily used by his friend and associate, Mileaway (James Cagney), whose street-wise slang and rapid vocal delivery will be put to better use in *The Public Enemy*. What is important in *Doorway to Hell*, a film that is sorely neglected in many scholarly accounts of the gangster genre, is that it secures the foundational image of the racketeer in early sound films that will be developed further by Warner Bros. and other studios.

Adapted from the 1929 novel by W.R. Burnett, *Little Caesar* firmly establishes the racketeer archetype in American cinema. Enrico Cesare Bandello (Edward G. Robinson) becomes the classic prototype for the rise-and-fall narrative structure of the racketeer who ascends from rural bandit to head of a criminal organization. According to Jack Shadoian, *Little Caesar* provides a '"poetics" of the gangster film. It is to the gangster film, what *Oedipus Rex*, in Aristotle's analysis, is to Greek tragedy' (2003: 34). Burnett himself referred to Rico as a 'gutter Macbeth – a composite figure that would indicate how men could rise to prominence or money under the most hazardous conditions' (quoted in McGilligan 1986: 57). This in itself implies a rise-and-fall structure that is immediately addressed in the opening sequences – the gas station robbery and the diner. The viewer only witnesses the robbery from a distance as shadowy figures leave an automobile and force the station attendant back into the building, gun shots are heard and a few moments later the figures scurry back to their car and leave. Much like the opening drive-by shooting in *Doorway to Hell*, the film begins with violent action. But prior to the action sequence the screenplay to *Little Caesar* opens with an epigram, a foreword from Machiavelli – 'The first law of every being is to preserve itself and live. You sow hemlock, and expect to see ears of corn ripen' (see Peary 1981: 45). This is replaced by Biblical verse in the film: 'For all that take up the sword shall perish with the sword' (Matthew 26:52). Machiavelli's advice is a more appropriate one from Rico's perspective – and is often reiterated in his dialogue in the diner. Its replacement with biblical verse seems tacked on to appease the censors with its 'crime does not pay' implication. In the historical context of Depression-era America, Rico becomes a symbol of survival through violent action or physical coercion, which is present from the opening sequence. The diner sequence establishes further indications of Rico's desire for status and his own self-importance via the newspaper headlines. Rico reads the news account of 'Diamond' Pete Montana and begins to compare himself to the mobster: 'I could do all *that* fellow does. More! When I get in a tight spot, I shoot my way out of it. Like tonight ... sure, shoot first – argue afterwards. If you don't the other feller gets you ... *This* game ain't for guys that's soft!' Shortly afterward, Rico expresses his own personal philosophy that initiates and motivates his rise to success in the underworld: 'Money's all right. But it ain't everything! Yeah – Be somebody! Look hard at a bunch of guys and know that they'll do what you tell'em. Have your own way or nuthin! ... Be somebody!' This motto becomes the *raison d'être* for not only Rico but every gangster to follow, and is the primary motivation for the racketeer in gangster cinema. Rico is defined throughout the film by his cockiness and aggressive behaviour. As he makes clear his desire for success is motivated primarily by power rather than material wealth. Indeed throughout the film Rico claims a Spartan existence devoid of women, liquor, and family. He is the lone individual and this codes him as an 'aberrant gangster ... representative as a force of chaos and excess who is in opposition to the structured organisation of the gang' (Mason 2002: 11). Rico's sense of self-importance is prevalent throughout the film as he climbs the ladder of criminal success and is most pronounced in his famous dying words when he refers to himself in the third person: 'Mother of Mercy, is this the end of Rico?'

In contrast to Rico's self-fulfilled desire 'to be somebody', Tom Powers (James Cagney) in *The Public Enemy* has no desire to make it big, but is rather more concerned with immediate gratifications and the material possessions that are acquired as a low-level enforcer. As the re-release foreword claims, the purpose of the film is to 'depict an environment ... rather than glorify the criminal'. It successfully characterises the un-heroic gangster, the street hoodlum whose success is depicted through his acquisition of material goods: clothes, automobiles, and women. As Richard Maltby confirms, Tom is 'more hoodlum than gangster, occupying a subordinate role in the bootlegging business, not an organizational one, obeying instructions rather than giving them, and untroubled by any ambition' (2005: 52). Yet Tom is not a lone individual like Rico; he is defined in relation to his family, his friend, as well as his gang associates (both Putty Nose's street gang and 'social club' and Paddy Ryan's bootlegging operation). These familial and societal relationships are illustrated by Tom's physical freedom. Fran Mason maintains that Tom is defined by his physical mobility in the urban space as an indication of his masculinity. He states that, 'the control of space becomes an expression of masculinity which becomes an index of identity in the film and its achievement is associated with creating a place for the self in [modern] society' (2002: 21). For the street hood this mastery of urban space is important in that it creates an identity for the gangster in the Depression-era world of prohibition. He achieves this through his physicality and his appropriation of material goods that help him navigate that space efficiently. Yet the gangster is doomed by his success and there comes a moment of self-recognition in the film where he realises that his power is limited. Much like Rico's dying words in *Little Caesar*, Tom's self-recognition comes after he has avenged the death of his friend Matt Doyle (Edward Woods), and wounded and stumbling along the rain-soaked city streets says, 'I ain't so tough!', before he falls into the gutter. Though this is not the end of the film, it represents a key moment where Tom questions his own masculinity and self-importance. Yet, as Mason states, it also reflects his 'audacity in going alone into a rival gang's headquarters' (2002: 22) and his self-image is fatally injured in the process. Another telling example of the temporality of life and material wealth is indicated in the title of the source novel for the film, *Beer and Blood*. Chicago writers John Bright and Kubec Glasmon based their novel partially on actual events and persons in Prohibition-era Chicago, drawing on such figures as Al Capone, Nails Morton, Hyman Weiss, and Louis 'Two-Gun' Alterie. On a metaphoric level the title 'Beer and Blood' suggests the profane, fleeting materiality of life through consumption and temporality while it also suggest an inversion of the sacrament (though religion plays no role in the book or the film) based on material possessions and not on spiritual wealth.

The Hays Office and the Outlaw

The second gangster archetype of the 1930s, the outlaw, can be viewed as the result of the confluence of three forces: the crime wave of the early 1930s, the Hays Office response to external pressure groups, and the process of Hollywood re-genrification. These forces created an archetype for a gangster-like character that is distinguishable from the racketeer primarily by his individualism, mobility, and temporal life style – a character who in many ways is representative of Depression-era America itself. But the edict from the Hays Office made clear that there would be no more sympathetic gangsters in Hollywood films, so he is now relegated to a secondary status as the film's antagonist. This in turn created a criminal character that could be utilised to reinforce the law-and-order narrative that helped reinvigorate the gangster genre in the mid-1930s with the valorisation of federal policing. The development of this outlaw figure as well as additional genre variations 'signaled important shifts in what the gangster would come to signify in the wartime and postwar era' (Munby 1999: 113). In this sense, it represents both a historical and cultural outgrowth of the gangster image as it develops in American cinema.

Clearly related to the outlaw bandits of the American West, in many respects, the outlaw gangster is a loner who typically controls a small gang of robbers in a rural environment, who make their living robbing small-town banks. The criminal focus here is on armed robbery as a professional activity rather than a large urban criminal syndicate operation such as bootlegging. The outlaw is also contrasted with the racketeer because he is of the people, a WASP American, devoid of the ethnic traits often associated with urban criminality. In this regard, the outlaw gangster figure invokes some of the attributes of historian Eric Hobsbawm's concept of the 'social bandit'. I say 'some of the attributes' because this archetype also develops over the years so that a character such as Duke Mantee in *The Petrified Forest* (1936) is considerably less sympathetic than Roy Earle in *High Sierra* (1941), though the same actor, Humphrey Bogart, portrays both of them. According to Hobsbawm, the social bandit represents or fights for the aspirations of the poor, the oppressed, and the socially disenfranchised:

> The point about social bandits is that they are peasant outlaws whom the lord and state regard as criminals, but who remain within peasant society, and are considered by their people as heroes, as champions, avengers, fighters for justice, perhaps even leaders of liberation, and in any case as men to be admired, helped and supported. (2000: 20)

In the mid-1930s, coming directly after the 'war on crime' by the federal government, one would be hard-pressed to find a sympathetic outlaw figure in American films. The outlaw gangster characters do possess some of these attributes and were often recognised as thinly-disguised versions of their real-life counterparts by critics and audiences alike. Another distinguishing characteristic of the outlaw archetype is his mobility. Unlike the racketeer, the outlaw is more mobile through his use of automobile technology. The automobile is not a signifier for material wealth and social status as it is for the racketeer, but is rather a means of business, transportation, survival, and escape. Cars are often stolen, and of temporary use, and an auto mechanic is always a significant part of the outlaw gang (as in the later *Bonnie and Clyde*). Automobiles, in this regard, are always a means to an end rather than vice versa. The automobile is also an indicator of the temporality of the outlaw gangster figure. The outlaw is notable for his lack of conspicuous consumption, rarely living in luxury or moving in fashionable social circles, spending most of his brief, action-driven life on the move or in hiding. The money that he acquires through robbery is often used for survival and day-to-day existence. Although the origins of the outlaw can be traced to such figures as Robin Hood, Jesse James, and the Younger Brothers, its historical context during the 1930s was the crime wave that occurred in the Midwest United States from 1932 to 1934.

The last stand of rugged individualism – the Depression-era outlaw: *The Petrified Forest* (1936)

Famous outlaw figures of the Depression years include Pretty Boy Floyd, Baby Face Nelson, Alvin Karpis and the Barker gang, Bonnie and Clyde, and the most notorious of them all, John Dillinger. Their exploits were well documented and fictionalised in newspapers, song, true crime magazines, radio, fiction, and film. As Carlos Clarens notes: 'The best-known cases came from the Midwest, whence sprang the new figure of the Depression desperado. This character, of almost pure American stock, was to displace the flashy, foreign, urban mobster from the front pages and to establish an affective rapport with the gunfighters of the Old West' (1980: 120). The ensuing crime wave instigated a federal policing response that valorised and mythologised the FBI in American culture, where the Depression-era desperados 'became prize trophies for the new FBI' (ibid.). Both the publicity and popularity of the celebrity bandits fomented not only a federal policing response but also a censorial response by moral guardians concerned with their influence on juvenile delinquency in the 1930s.

Throughout the early 1930s the content of gangster films was negotiated through the Hays Office. In 1930 the Production Code was adopted by the film industry as a means of self-regulation in response to what was seen as objectionable content in motion pictures and subsequent censorship by local and state censorship boards. The Code established 'General Principles' and 'Particular Applications' that addressed the depiction of sex, crime, vice, and violence on screen. Though it was adopted by the industry it was not strictly enforced until 1934 when Joseph Breen became the head of the Production Code Administration (PCA) and began to closely monitor studio productions beginning at the script level. As a result of the Payne Fund studies (1929–33) to investigate the influence of motion pictures on young audiences, several specific studies focused on the depiction of crime on screen and its subsequent influence on juvenile delinquency. Much of the testimonial examples included many specific references to gangster film, particularly the lavish lifestyle of on-screen gangsters and the educational effects of crime films. For example, one male youth, who was working off a burglary sentence, admitted that watching gangster pictures created the desire 'to always have plenty of money and ride around in swell machines, wear good clothes, and grab a girl whenever you wanted – I still think it would be a great life!'; another Chicago youngster stated, 'seeing gangsters having lots of money and big cars and being big shots makes a fellow want them' (quoted in Forman 1935: 185). These testimonials and others were used by the studies to draw a connection between the films themselves and juvenile crime. The investigators also looked on motion pictures as creating a 'curriculum of crime' by showing criminal activities on screen. 'The movies are a school, a system of education virtually unlimited, untrammeled, and uncontrolled' opined one of the studies related to movies, delinquency, and crime. At one point the investigator provides a laundry list of examples of the educational effects of gangster films: how to open a safe by 'feel' of the dial; how to enter a store by forcing a lock with crowbar and screwdriver; how to jimmy a door or window; the use of gloves in burglary; how to sell liquor in a 'booze racket' by coercion; carrying a machine gun in a violin case.

In the same study one juvenile felon readily admitted, 'I learned something from "The Doorway to Hell!" It is how to drown out shots from a gun by backfiring a car!' (quoted in Forman 1935: 203). The motion picture industry was not only besieged by the results of the Payne Fund studies themselves but also by several organised women's groups such as the Parents and Teachers Association, the General Federation of Women's Clubs, and others who wanted stricter enforcement of the Production Code. Coupled with the threat of boycotts of motion pictures by the influential Catholic Legion of Decency, the MPAA acquiesced by forming the Production Code Administration in 1934. Coincident to the establishment of the PCA and its new administrator, Joseph Breen, was the killing of John Dillinger by the FBI as he was leaving the Biograph Theatre in Chicago on 22 July 1934. Prior to the death of Dillinger and motivated by media accounts of his activities, Will Hays stipulated in a telegram to Breen that

> No motion picture on the life or exploits of John Dillinger will be produced, distributed or exhibited by any member [of the MPAA] ... This decision is based on the belief that the production, distribution or exhibition of such a picture could be detrimental to the best public interest. Action supporting this decision has been taken by the Executive Committee of this Association. Please advise all studio heads accordingly. (1934)

Although there was an edict from the PCA not to produce films based on the life of John Dillinger, a cycle of crime films were produced valorising the exploits of the G-Men, the federal agents responsible for Dillinger's death. Beginning with Warner Bros.' *G-Men* with James Cagney and continuing through such films as *Public Hero #1* (MGM, 1935), *Let Em' Have It* (UA, 1935), *Show Them No Mercy* (Twentieth Century Fox, 1935), *Men Without Names* (Paramount, 1935) and *Bullets or Ballots* (Warner Bros., 1936) these films often fictionalised the exploits and historical incidents of real outlaws, particularly John Dillinger. The outlaw gangster figure becomes prominent during this period because of his ability to circumnavigate the PCA restrictions by playing a secondary role of victim rather than victimiser. In many of these films, incidents from the Dillinger crime wave were indirectly referenced such as the prison jail break, the gang's hide-out at the Little Bohemia Lodge, the use of plastic surgery to disguise facial recognition, a gang member who is also a doctor, and automotive mobility to elude capture. Perhaps the most direct reference to Dillinger occurs in *Public Hero #1* when the outlaw Sonny Black (Joseph Calleia), who has undergone plastic surgery, hides out temporarily in a crowded vaudeville theatre and is subsequently gunned down by federal agents upon leaving. The *New York Times* review of the film noted the similarities:

Fancifully related to the exploits of the late Mr. Dillinger ... the film describes the last frantic days of a gunman between the time of his escape from prison and his assassination under the spitting guns of the Department of Justice. ... You must recall that Dillinger spent his last hour watching a gangster picture in a movie house. The producers, anxious to capitalize on this now historic episode, but also fearful that by enacting it truthfully they might provide ammunition for the foes of the cinema, have located the business in a two-a-day house. (Sennewald 1935: 12)

With the growing concern that the G-man films were still exploiting the gangster outlaw and the violent events of recent history and the rejecting of a number of these films by the UK and Canada, Joseph Breen suggested to Will Hays lessening the large number of criminal activities involving organised gangs in crime films, saying that, 'crime stories are not acceptable when they portray the activities of American gangsters armed and in violent conflict with the law or law-enforcement officers' (Hays 1935). These actions illustrate how volatile the depiction of organised gang activities remained even when the studios were creating variations on a theme for the cinematic gangster.

Surviving the Hays Office: Generic Mobility in the Gangster Film

Much of the scholarship on the gangster film has focused on the early 'classic' gangster films formalisation of the genre and the studio-imposed repression as a result of the enforcement of the Production Code. Subsequently, the genre became fragmented into other sub-genres such as the G-Man cycle of the mid-1930s. Thomas Schatz, for example, claims that 'the gangster film enjoyed possibly the briefest classic period of any Hollywood genre. Its evolution was severely disrupted by external social forces, and its narrative formula was splintered into various derivative strains' (1981: 82). Likewise, Christine Gledhill notes the fragmentation of the gangster film that was 'enumerated in terms of various cycles, phases and subgenres: the G-Man cycle, *film noir*, crime melodramas and so on' (1985: 279). And Robert Warshow's seminal work is focused primarily on the classic gangster film, particularly *Little Caesar* and *The Public Enemy*, in distinguishing its primary genre characteristics. When MoMA built its film library the one gangster film that it immediately acquired instantly received canonical status, *The Public Enemy*. Due to the Breen office edict on re-issues receiving a seal of approval, many of the gangster films of the early 1930s lapsed into an almost contraband existence – the void of forgotten films. This contributed to the canonisation of films that were immediately available. What remains a historiographic problem in regards to the gangster film is the fact that there was already fragmentation of the genre occurring in its classic period. The rise-and-fall narrative is only applicable to a few (very few) films. In 1930/31 alone there were gangster comedies (*Hook, Line and Sinker*), rum running films (*Corsair*), gambling films (*Smart Money*), rival bootleg families and their 'star-crossed' lovers *à la* Romeo and Juliet (*The Guilty Generation*), vigilante films (*The Secret Six*), and witness intimidation films (*The Star Witness*). The one common factor among all of these films is that they concern racketeering as a major plot line and the gangster as racketeer as a major character. It should also be pointed out that many actors that portrayed racketeers during the 'classic' cycle are not immediately associated with the genre: Clark Gable, Spencer Tracy, Wallace Beery, Boris Karloff, John Gilbert. Fran Mason points out the importance of these diverse gangster forms when he notes that 'in many ways these films [*Quick Millions*, *Three on a Match*, *Taxi!*, *Smart Money*, *Blondie Johnson*] are as important as the classic cycle because they form models or sub-genres which are returned to, in modified form, in later years' (2002: 31). Mason also stipulates that the classic films as a variation of the gangster genre may have inadvertently received their canonical status because the Breen office moratorium on gangster films curtailed the further development of the genre. What becomes important here is that the fragmentation of the genre is part of its development and is indelibly linked to representation. The generic mobility of the gangster is exemplified in variations including the Dual Gangster (good/evil) in films such a *The Roaring Twenties* (1940), a comic variant – the Runyonesque gangster (*A Slight Case of Murder* (1938), *All Through the Night* (1942)) and the fish-out-of-water comic variant in films such as *Hideout* (1934) and *Brother Orchid* (1940). There are numerous others as the representations of the gangster are also utilised in series film entries (Dick Tracy, Torchy Blane, Boston Blackie, and so on) and in other film cycles. Two examples will be discussed here to provide an indication of both a generic variation and a film cycle created in response to historical/ topical events: the horror gangster variant and the 'Crusading D.A.' films.

Black Friday (1940) is a Universal studio B-film starring Boris Karloff that combines elements of both the horror film and the gangster film. It personifies the gangster as 'monster' in its rather simplistic plot involving a brain transplant with the standard melodramatic consequences of such a procedure. The story concerns Professor George Kingsley (Stanley Ridges), a teacher of English literature at a small-town college, who becomes the victim of an automobile accident involving rival gangsters, one of whom, Red Cannon, is also injured. Dr. Ernest Sovac (Karloff), Kinglsey's friend, decides to perform an operation to save Kingsley's life that involves transplanting Cannon's brain into Kingsley's body. The rest of the film revolves around the Jekyll/Hyde-style transformations that take place as a result and the revenge killings of Cannon's fellow gangster associates. The interest here is the demonization of the gangster-as-monster in the film. This transformation utilises many of the narrative tropes and representational elements in gangster films to create the gangster as demonic 'other'. When Kingsley becomes Red Cannon (usually instigated by the noise of a siren) he takes on a different vocalisation that utilises the colorful argot associated with the genre. His appearance also becomes more stylised and dapper compared to the rather absent-minded and mundane appearance of the professor. The trailer for the film, which establishes essential genre traits that audiences would recognise, makes the comparison quite clear. The tag line 'New Horror Fills the Screen' suggests something innovative in the Universal release. The trailer voice-over explicitly states the major plot device for the film and the 'new horror' that audiences will encounter: 'Into the body of a gentle scholar is grafted the brain of a criminal ... and a new and deadly monster is born to ravage an unsuspecting world'. Short clips follow from scenes depicting the gangster/monster wreaking havoc. *Black Friday* illustrates an interesting and short-lived variant of the gangster film that utilises generic elements from two genres to create a gangster-as-monster variation, much like the brain grafting that occurs in the film.

Generic variations will become a standard practice of the gangster genre and continues through such contemporary variations as the mob comedy, Mafia films, hit man films, and witness protection films. Another way the gangster film develops is in relation to topicality through production cycles. These cycles best exemplify the gangster films 'symbiotic relation to contemporary events' (Gledhill 1985: 279). One such short-lived cycle (and they are contained cycles because of the temporary 'newsworthy' nature of their events) was the 'crusading DA cycle' or as some trade journals referred to it 'the Dewey cycle' of 1937/38 instigated by the topicality of Thomas E. Dewey and his crime-fighting efforts against the rackets. Working as special prosecutor in New York during the mid-1930s, Thomas Dewey specifically targeted underworld figures such as Dutch Schultz, Louis 'Lepke' Buchalter (the head of Murder, Incorporated that was designed to eliminate many of the witnesses and suspected informants that Dewey was using) and Charles 'Lucky' Luciano for prosecution. In June 1936 he successfully indicted and convicted Luciano on racketeering charges.[3] As a result of the newsworthiness of this event, Hollywood responded almost immediately with a cycle of films that used the circumstances of the trial and the crimes as the basis for fictional storylines. Films such as *Smashing the Vice Trust* (Real Life Dramas, 1937), *Marked Woman* (Warner Bros., 1937), *Counsel for Crime* (Columbia, 1937), *Racket Busters* (Warner Bros., 1938), *Smashing the Rackets* (RKO, 1938), *I Am the Law* (Columbia, 1938), and *Crime Takes a Holiday* (Columbia, 1938) featured a crusading district attorney who was investigating racketeering in the big city. These films also used the racketeer image for the gangster protagonists and often featured the way racketeers victimised the American public through extortion and intimidation. This brief film cycle indicates how the gangster film relied not only on generic variations but on contemporaneous news events to survive the restrictions imposed upon it by the Production Code during the studio era.

Notes

1   The cultural image of Capone was also a contemporary one to the 1920s and 1930s. This is evidenced by a questionnaire that was used for one of the Payne Fund Studies, 'Movies, Deliquency, and Crime' by Herbert Blumer and Philip M. Hauser. The name 'Al Capone' is directly referenced on two items, '15. Show by an X which of the following are good men, and by an O which are bad men' and '16. Show by a check mark which you would like to be. If you are a girl, indicate which you would like to have as your friends.' In both categories Capone is one of the choices, followed by George Bancroft (who portrayed Bull Weed in *Underworld*), Lon Chaney (who portrayed a host of criminals onscreen), Tom Mix, and Hack Wilson (an American Major League

baseball player for the Chicago Cubs from 1926 to 1931). Al Capone is also directly referenced by John Barrymore in Warner Bros.' early sound film *Show of Shows* (1929) in his brief introduction to a soliloquy from Shakespeare's *Henry VI, Part One* when he describes the character of Richard, the Duke of Gloucester (who would later become King Richard III), by comparing his murderous exploits to the 'graceful impartiality of Al Caponi'.

2   In addition to Gancy (1995) see also John Sedgwick and Michael Pokorny, 'The Risk Environment of Film Making: Warner Bros. in the Inter-War Years', *Explorations in Economic History*, 35 (1998): 196–220, for further discussion of the economic performance of the studio in the early Depression years.

3   For more information on the crime-busting career of Thomas E. Dewey see Mary M. Stolberg (1995) *Fighting Organized Crime: Politics, Justice and the Legacy of Thomas E. Dewey*. Boston: Northeastern University Press and Albert Fried (1993) *The Rise and Fall of the Jewish Gangster in America*. New York: Columbia University Press.

3 MURDER, INCORPORATED: POST-WAR DEVELOPMENTS IN THE GANGSTER FILM

> Mobsters looked like business executives, lived in the same neighborhoods, contributed to political campaigns, and acted like good citizens – all with the goal of sinking their tentacles into 'legitimate enterprises'. Their appearance and taste did not immediately connote difference and inferiority. Indeed, the gangster's affinity for mainstream and elite practices was what seemed most frightening to the Kefauver Committee and its many viewers.
>
> Lee Bernstein, *The Greatest Menace* (2002: 71)

As we have seen thus far, the development of the gangster film in American cinema is closely connected to topical criminal events such as the concern over urban crime in the Progressive era, gangsters of the Prohibition era, and the Depression outlaws of the mid-1930s. The topicality of gangsters and outlaws and their concomitant glorification in the mass media, particularly film, gave rise to the suppression of sympathetic criminal images and the fragmentation of the genre into hybrids and sub-genres in the late 1930s. The 1940s and 1950s witnessed further fragmentation of the gangster film that developed along three distinct paths: the *noir* gangster, the syndicate film, and the retro-gangster film. These subgenres originated with the topicality of two events in particular: the Murder, Incorporated trials of 1940/41 and the Kefauver Crime Committee hearings in 1950/51. Both events were well publicised by the press and re-invoked in the public's eye the criminal activities of prominent gangsters of yesteryear. In 1947, Al Capone died and the PCA reiterated its ban on gangster bio-pics fearing an onslaught of films based on the life of the most notorious of the Prohibition-era gangsters.[1] These true crime events also helped create a conspiracy theory of organised crime whose octopus-like tentacles were supposedly far reaching into American society and business. In addition they fostered a cultural image of organised crime as a corporate empire that in the words of Hyman Roth in *The Godfather, Part II* (1978) was 'bigger than US Steel'. This image of the syndicate crime organisation considerably affected the gangster film, whose representation of the gangster's loss of individuality was a central part of the post-war era. Ideological and thematic developments in the genre increasingly emphasised the loss of individuality and the alienation of the gangster, who is now 'cut adrift from any sense of social or communal coherence or identity' (Mason 2002: 73). This alienation of self will become a prominent thematic motif in not only post-war gangster films but also the films of Francis Ford Coppola, Martin Scorsese, and even more contemporary gangster films and is a significant factor in its development as a genre.

These variations show how the gangster essentially becomes a conceptual image in order to examine larger cultural issues taking place in post-war America. These variations are also significant because of their industrial context as primarily independent productions. Independent production would gradually become more important after the Paramount decree that forced the major studios to divest their large theatre chains and as a consequence cut back on production. Part of this cut back effort was the way post-war independent production companies subsumed the elimination of 'B' film production by the major studios. The crime film proved very lucrative in this regard because of its economics. As Jonathan Munby notes,

> The crime film was both topical and low-budget. It was amenable to cost-saving devices, such as location shooting, use of everyday fashion, low-key high-contrast lighting (which saved on expensive set design and costumes), and long takes (which saved on film stock). Not surprisingly, at war's end, the crime film emerged as a prized venue for newly independent studios and for quasi-independent offshoots of the majors, which included Enterprise Studios

... Cagney Productions, John Huston's Horizon Production Company, Hal Wallis Productions, and Mark Hellinger's International Pictures. Significantly, all of the latter were composed of film talent once associated with Warner Brothers' crime and social problem films. (1999: 124)

Throughout the 1950s independent production became the norm for crime pictures, particularly gangster films, culminating in the cycle of retro-gangster films that began with Don Siegel's *Baby Face Nelson* (1957). But before discussing the gangster variations that will be the central focus for this chapter, it is necessary to discuss a film that was released in 1945 and is in many ways a precursor to the post-war developments in the American gangster film in regards to its industrial and thematic context.

The Return of the Repressed: The King Brothers' Dillinger (1945)

The 1945 release of the King Brothers' film *Dillinger*, starring Lawrence Tierney, is generally regarded as somewhat of an anomaly by many film scholars. It was a very successful 'B' film from Monogram Pictures (that produced nothing but 'B' films in the studio era) that marked a return to the genre's roots in topicality. Carlos Clarens, for instance, claimed that through cost-cutting efforts the gangster genre 'had been distilled to its essence' and that *Dillinger* 'may have been the first conceptual gangster epic' (1980: 190). And Jack Shadoian, as many other scholars have done, briefly notes that the film 'stands alone, filling the gap between the Code's prohibition against the gangster as the central figure and the mid-1950s to early 1960s cycle' of gangster biographies' (2003: 27) whereas, Fran Mason views the film as a return to the 'big shot narratives' that empha-sized the 'violent bodily gangster reliant on his strength and willpower' (2002: 64). Typically only briefly mentioned in these historical accounts of the gangster film, *Dillinger* is most often relegated to the status of a curiosity. What becomes intriguing is the circumstances of its production. Why and how was it able to be produced and distributed at all, when Will Hays and Joseph Breen were opposed to film biographies of gangsters (and specifically, per the 1934 telegram, films concerning John Dillinger)? In fact, Breen himself gave the film the PCA certification that enabled it to be distributed in 1945. The answer to that question becomes apparent when one examines both the historical context of the film's production, the film itself, and how it was able to negotiate Code restrictions through narrative acquiescence.

Many accounts of *film noir* note the significance of the production and release of *Double Indemnity* (1944), a crime thriller based on the novel by James M. Cain. First published in serial form in 1936, its publication as a novel in 1943 followed the surge in paperback publishing during the war years. The screen adaptation of the novel by Billy Wilder and Raymond Chandler often relied on innuendo and verbal wit in the dialogue to circumvent Code restrictions. The Production Code itself was loosening its strictures somewhat because of the war. Sheri Biesen connects the circumstances of PCA laxity to wartime production – when scripts and films were subject to Office of War Information (OWI) interference as well as Office of Censorship standards that often contradicted Code restrictions. Biesen also claims that Breen's 'brief sojourn at RKO [as general manager] – providing a brief lapse in his rigorous administering of the PCA between 1941 and 1942 – may well have affected his previous by-the-book approach to Code enforcement ... producing a more temperate censor in 1943 than in 1935' (2005: 103). At any account, *Double Indemnity*, considered one of the classic *noir* films, was able to obtain a Seal of Approval by the PCA, though changes were made in order for it to do so.

Perhaps even more significant in regard to the King Bros. production of *Dillinger*, was 20th Century-Fox's 1944 release of *Roger Touhy, Gangster!*, a film based on incidents from the life of Roger Touhy (1898–1957), one of Capone's rival bootleggers. The film was produced in April/May 1943 shortly after Touhy's escape from the Stateville Federal Penitentiary on 9 October 1942. It allowed for a 'crime does not pay' moral judgment through its use of both a written foreword appearing before the opening credits that acknowledged the co-operation of institutional authorities and the fact that other than Touhy and his gang all other characters were fictitious and an afterword that featured the on-screen appearance of Statesville Prison Warden Joseph H. Ragen, who had allowed filming inside the prison. Ragen adds the moral dictum in his brief remarks:

They say crime doesn't pay. I disagree – crime does pay. It pays off in disgrace to yourself and family – and for those who continue to disregard law and order even while in prison, this is the only answer – solitary confinement. I wish that every man, woman, and child in America could see for themselves just how a person who has lived outside the law lives behind prison bars. I would much rather see you here as a visitor than as a permanent guest of the State of Illinois.

This brief statement was added to the film after photography was completed in order to appease the Office of Censorship. Although it was provided with a PCA certificate for exhibition on 4 December 1947, it was declared 'unsuitable for re-release or re-issue' following the death of Al Capone and the subsequent MPAA ban on gangster films based on real criminals.

The King Brothers produced *Dillinger* in October 1944 and it was released in early March 1945. The film conveys a very unsympathetic gangster in the characterisation of John Dillinger. Tierney unrealistically portrays the outlaw as a cold-blooded, sadistic, sociopath where many of his crimes are committed for vengeance and personal motives. The film opens with newsreel footage in a small movie theatre recounting the violent exploits of Dillinger. His father is introduced by the theatre manager and he tells the audience about his son's early childhood in Indiana. This opening foreword segues into Dillinger's first crime – the robbery of a small grocer, which lands him in prison. The further exploits of the Depression-era's most famous outlaw are then dramatised through the course of the film. The film is important in the post-war development of the gangster film primarily because of its status as an independent production that featured the return of the gangster as protagonist and its spectacle of violence. The violence is brutal – a mutilation by broken glass, a cold-blooded shooting of one of the gang members in front of the gang, and even an axe murder – all by Dillinger's hands. Although the film received Code certification for release and was quite popular it was not without its critics, who were vehement in their remarks.

According to Jonathan Munby, who deals more extensively with *Dillinger* and its unique importance to the gangster film than most scholars, 'the general premise the producers used to "sell" the film to the Code Administration to gain its Seal of Approval for general release was to argue that *Dillinger* gave its audience a classic example of how "crime does not pay"' (1999: 152). The film primarily accomplishes this through its unsympathetic gangster protagonist and the narrative-framing device of the film's prologue 'this too could happen to your son' testimonial sequence. However, following its release, *Dillinger* was attacked for re-igniting the dormant controversy over the gangster film itself. According to the PCA files part of the critical attacks on the film were concerns that it would initiate another cycle of gangster pictures and influence adolescent viewers with their depictions of crime and its promise of instant gratification. As reported by one newspaper account, a woman wrote claiming that:

> Now that we've had the life of Dillinger on the screen – with what Hollywood considers good box-office results – I suppose we'll have a cycle of gangster pictures inflicted on us once more ... Hollywood will justify itself by concluding each picture on a 'crime does not pay' note. But the kids will puff their reefers and swagger defiantly that 'it was fun while it lasted'. (Quoted in Munby 1999: 154)

These claims make manifest the still ongoing concern with civic and moral responsibility and the need for censorship of gangster imagery – especially in the form of film biographies of notorious criminals. Equally illuminating is the response by film director Frank Borzage who contextualised the threat of *Dillinger* very differently. In a letter to the MPAA concerning the film, Borzage invoked the potential harm another cycle of gangster films would create:

> I have viewed with growing alarm the trend towards another cycle of gangster and racketeer films. Nothing can do this country and the motion picture industry more harm at this particular time than films designed to glamorize gangsters and their way of life.
>
> At present our entire nation is working desperately on a plan, which will bring peace and prosperity and good will to all the world. Foreign nations are looking to the U.S. for guidance. Much of that guidance and influence we will wield on the outside world will be transmitted through the medium of the motion picture.
>
> This is certainly an inopportune time for us to convey the impression that America is made up largely of gangsters, black market operators, petty racketeers and murderers. (Quoted in Munby 1999: 149)

Borzage is obviously concerned with a post-war American environment and the reflection motion pictures will make to foreign markets. Referencing not only gangster films but also the rise in *noir* crime films, these remarks address the still-volatile issue of the image of gangster criminals, particularly when they are the central characters in films, which Borzage directly addresses later: 'Here the motion picture industry has the opportunity to help stamp out this crime wave before it begins. The first step is the total elimination of the glamorized gangster movies' (quoted in Munby 1999: 156). Though a cycle of gangster biopics did not develop during this period, a de-glamorisation of the gangster did occur in several *noir* films produced in the post-war era.

The Noir Gangster

As a post-war development the *noir* gangster is characterised by his status as both a gangster protagonist and an angst-ridden male *noir* criminal. The *noir* gangster is indicative of the post-war cultural change in America from an independent, self-sustaining nation into a corporate global power. As Andrew Spicer notes, the *noir* gangster 'is no longer the dynamic, brash, confident entrepreneur of the prewar cycle, but [is] riddled with existential neuroses' (2002: 88). He is often an alienated figure who either lashes out at the world through violence (Cody Jarrett in *White Heat* (1949)), or is unsure of his place in an increasingly changing and corporate-style environment *(The Gangster* (1947), *I Walk Alone* (1948)). Fran Mason suggests that the new postwar society is part of the figuration of the *noir* gangster: 'Where the classic gangster film represented the gangster straining against social restrictions and finding that individuality was only possible outside official society in the world of criminality, the films of the early post-war years represent new power alignments where the individual gangster is often straining to assert his desires against the limits imposed by the gang' (2002: 73). The gang has now become a syndicate – a corporate criminal enterprise that is a part of society and therefore functions as an impersonal business enterprise. The result is that the *noir* gangster is now an outsider, an alienated individual who is riddled by anxieties and paranoia that characterise many *noir* protagonists of the 1940s. Often portrayed as a psychopath, the *noir* gangster's male anxieties are indicative of post-war male traumas that are only alleviated through physical violence and the infliction of pain on others. This is one aspect of the *noir* gangster that is best evidenced in films such as *White Heat, Kiss of Death* (1947), and *Kiss Tomorrow Goodbye* (1950). Another perhaps more significant aspect of the *noir* gangster protagonist is his passive emasculated masculinity.

The *noir* gangster closely relates to the way masculinity is represented in the 'tough' thrillers – a classification that critic Frank Krutnik uses to categorise the representation of masculinity in certain *noir* films. Though he does not specify gangster *noir* in particular, Krutnik's conceptualisation of masculinity in the 'tough thriller' category contains many attributes of the *noir* gangster figure. According to Krutnik, the 'tough thriller' is characterised by the depiction of masculine failure, powerlessness, and impairment. As opposed to the investigative thriller with typically a hard-boiled detective as protagonist, the 'tough' thriller often presents 'an erosion of confidence in the legitimizing framework of masculine authority, marked in the film by the cultural systems of law, business, and family' (1991: 128). Krutnik uses the term 'paranoid man' films to describe their narrative focus as 'melodramas … concerned with the problems besetting masculine identity and meaning. [Where] "tough", controlled masculinity becomes an ideal which is lost or unattainable' (1991: 131). The *noir* gangster is often presented as an emotionally fractured, emasculated male who is uncertain of his place within the social environment.

Gordon Wiles' *The Gangster* presents a classic *noir* gangster protagonist in the character of Shubunka (Barry Sullivan), a racketeer who operates on the boardwalk of Neptune Beach in New York City. Shubunka's racketeering operations are about to be taken over by a rival gang, representative of a forceful modern combination. But as the setting of Neptune Beach itself suggests, this is not the typical urban-centred location of the gangster film. Fran Mason discusses the importance of space in regard to the gangster film by noting that the classic gangster is typically in control of space through a process of territorialisation that he occupies in his urban environment. This is manifest in the film through his mobility, both bodily and through technological means (automobiles, trucks and so on). Whereas, the *noir* gangster is 'part of a process of deterritorialisation in which his identity is not expressed through the extension across space, but dissipated by it, existing in "liminal uncertainty"' (2002: 77). Shubunka is a racketeer who controls small-time operations along the beachfront amusement boardwalk. His primary hangout is an ice cream parlour and soda fountain owned by Nick Jammey (Akim Tamiroff) who pays Shubunka for protection. When we first see Shubunka he is alone in his apartment lying on a bed, completely motionless, not answering the phone calls from Jammey, simply existing off his racketeering efforts. Spatial design in the film is claustrophobic, exemplifying the liminal environment that the *noir* gangster inhabits. Shubunka's apartment is tightly shot, a large Daumier print hanging on the wall, the other part of the room almost catacomb-like with clothing drawers embedded in the wall. Even Shubunka's bed is small – nothing like the opulent four-poster beds typical of the material wealth of gangster life. The cramped space of Neptune Beach is shot con-servatively so as not to reveal its economic production values (it is another King Brothers Monogram release). As Martha Nochimson states, 'there is a sense of a pitiless depthlessness emanating from the candy store and Shubunka's apartment which is augmented by the blatant artificiality of the sets' (2007: 119). This is the deterritorialised space that the *noir* gangster inhabits – a confined, smothering environment that effectively paralyses his physicality and his ability to control space.

Shubunka's opening voice-over reveals his alienated status as well as his own justification for his existence:

> That was what I was referring to [the Daumier art print]. I worked the rackets, dirty rackets, ugly rackets. I was no hypocrite. I know what I did was low and rotten. I know what people think of me. What difference did it make ... what do I care? I got scarred sure [*the camera reveals his face in close-up and the scar on his cheek*] ... you get hurt a little when you fight your way out of a gutter. ... Neptune Beach, cheap concessionaires, grubby little storekeepers ... I made my money off them. Why shouldn't I? I despised them. I trusted nobody. I pulled myself out. I made good and my conscience never bothered me. I had nothing to be ashamed of ... nothing to fear.

He has several similar speeches throughout the film that are marked by the repetitive use of phrases that are used essentially as self-confirmations of his existential nature. Towards the end of the film, Shubunka seeks shelter at the home of Dorothy, the cashier at the soda shop, who despises the gangster. He knows that he is about to be killed by rival gangsters. After she lets Shubunka know how she feels he slowly turns to her saying:

The noir gangster as angst-ridden anti-hero: *The Gangster* (1947)

You understood nothing. You're sweet, and lovely, and good. You're also very young. Pay for my sins! You know what my sins were. I'll tell you – that I wasn't low enough. That I wasn't mean, and rotten, and dirty enough! That's right! I shoulda smashed Cornell first! I shoulda hounded Jammey – kept after him. Killed him myself! I shoulda trusted no one. Never had a friend! Never loved a woman! That's the way the world is. Wait. Live. Find out for yourself. That's the way you have to be – the only way!

Shubunka's ability for self-recognition through his monologues is unique among gangster protagonists and presents an attempt to justify his lack of certainty and action throughout the film. If Rico Bandello and Tony Camonte are often regarded as tragic, almost Shakespearean heroes, by contrast, Shubunka is clearly the Willy Loman of gangster films. The world has passed him by, and he has essentially become a racketeer without a racket. The *noir* gangster often fails to recognise, or recognises too late, the now dehumanised world that surrounds him. Gordon Wiles' film demythologises the gangster protagonist as a marginalised figure trying to survive in an increasingly complicated modernised world. This new gangster environment becomes more clearly defined by the emergence of the syndicate film in the 1950s.

The Syndicate Film

On 5 January 1950, Estes Kefauver, the Democratic senator from Tennessee, introduced Senate Resolution 202, calling for an investigation of organised crime in the United States. Kefauver had closely studied recent reports from crime commissions in California, Michigan, and Illinois and believed that the federal government needed to play an active role in assisting local governments with what he saw as a national problem. The purpose of the committee was threefold: to make a complete investigation to determine whether organised crime utilised the facilities of interstate commerce; to investigate the manner and extent of criminal operations that were taking place and identify the persons, firms, or corporations involved; and to determine whether such criminal operations were developing corrupting influences in violation of state or federal laws. The most important criminal activity that interested the committee was gambling and the use of the wire service by organised crime. At one point Kefauver made the claim that 'the Public Enemy No. One in America today is the Continental Press Agency': wire services broadcast racing news and other gambling information across many states, and the receipt of this information provided the basis for many large syndicate gambling operations.[2]

Within its fourteen-month duration (May 1950–July 1951) the committee travelled to fourteen cities and interviewed more than 700 witnesses, resulting in 12,000 pages of public testimony. Kefauver's motive for travelling around the country was primarily to show evidence of the extent of organised crime's influence across the nation. All of the cities the committee visited were large urban centres: Miami, Kansas City, St. Louis, Philadelphia, Chicago, Tampa, Cleveland, Detroit, New Orleans, Las Vegas, San Francisco, Los Angeles, Saratoga, and New York City. The committee hearings in New York generated the most publicity and were viewed as the climax to the proceedings. Several of the hearings had been televised on a local level. The New York hearings, however, were broadcast nationally, sponsored by *Time* magazine. Some of the most colourful witnesses testified during these hearings: Frank Costello, the reputed 'Prime Minister of the Underworld'; Virginia Hill Hausen, 'Mistress to the Mob' (who after her testimony told reporters, 'I hope an atom bomb drops on you!'); Ambassador William O'Dwyer, the former mayor of New York; Albert Anastasia, alleged boss of Murder, Inc.; and Jacob 'Greasy Thumb' Guzik.

The Kefauver Committee Report on Organized Crime was the official document that presented the results of the transcontinental investigation. The report concluded that organised crime existed on a national level: 'Organized criminal gangs operating in interstate commerce are firmly entrenched in our large cities in the operation of many different gambling enterprises such as bookmaking, policy, slot machines, as well as other rackets such as the sale and distribution of narcotics and commercialized prostitution'. Further, the report suggested that a 'sinister criminal organisation known as the Mafia' was the 'binder which ties together the two major criminal syndicates as well as numerous other criminal groups throughout the country'. The national organization of crime, the committee stated, wielded considerable power and constituted a shadow government that regulated its own trade, enforced its own laws, and used the laws of the legitimate government to further its interests. Yet the true significance of the committee was elsewhere. According to John Gorman, 'the significance of the hearings lay not so much in the quantity of evidence gathered by the committee as in the incredibly effective manner in which it managed to arouse an interest among great masses of people in the nature and scope of the problem of organized crime and its relationship to political corruption' (1971: 78). Hollywood producers were quick to capitalize on the topicality of organised crime in the nation's newspaper headlines by reinvigorating the relatively dormant gangster genre with 'Kefauverism'.

Early syndicate films released during the existence of the Kefauver Committee share several characteristics that set them apart from other crime films. Because of the widespread publicity and popularity of the hearings, the public became familiar with names and terms that eventually spilled over into popular culture. Key concepts of the committee hearings were utilised by Hollywood to invigorate crime films with topical references, either within the film's narrative or in a film's advertising. Syndicate films are concerned primarily with organised crime and its activities (gambling, bookmaking, and so on). Organised crime, therefore, becomes a key narrative element within these films, displacing the traditional gangster narrative form that centred on an individual protagonist. The early syndicate films also show a tendency to be explicatory in defining new terms and concepts of criminal activities (for example, 'the $2 bet' and other betting terms, a *hit*, a *contract*, and so forth). Also, these films tend to show crime as a business enterprise. A collective term is generally utilised, often in the film titles themselves, to describe the nebulous far-reaching criminal organizations: *The Mob* (1951), *Hoodlum Empire* (1952), *Chicago Syndicate* (1955) and *The System* (1955). Organized crime in these films is often referred to as 'the mob', 'the syndicate', or 'the combination'. As Jonathan Munby notes, 'these films focused on the decline of individual agency before the power of organizations, collectively reflecting the inquisition climate of the Red Scare that had only exacerbated the general paranoia about institutional power' (1999: 133).

Hoodlum Empire, released by Republic Pictures a year after the Kefauver hearings, contained numerous references to the crime commit-tee and is indicative of the genre characteristics of the syndicate film. Although real names are not used, reviewers pointed out the similarities between characters in the film and their real-life counterparts. The *New York Times* review began by saying: 'It is fairly safe to state that the paying customers are bound to recognize similarities between *Hoodlum Empire*, now at the Globe, and a certain Senatorial investigation into crime, which also had some entertainment values' (Weiler 1952: 23). *Variety,* referring to *Hoodlum Empire* as a 'film version of the Kefauver investigation', stated that the

> film industry's pat foreword, events and characters depicted herein are purely imaginary ... which generally accompanies title credits of every picture, must be taken with a grain of salt insofar as *Hoodlum Empire* is concerned. For [Luther] Adler plays Frank Costello, [Brian] Donleavy [sic] recreates Sen. Kefauver and Miss [Claire] Trevor does a Virginia Hill down to the original camera-smashing incident. ... Others who stand out are Gene Lockhart, whose use of senatorial rhetoric closely resem-bles the style of Sen. Tobey. (1952: 6)

In addition to the narrative parallels to committee members and witnesses (Mancani/Costello; Stephens/Kefauver; Connie William/Virginia Hill), *Hoodlum Empire* provided information and revelations from the investiga-

The gangster as CEO pointing out the extent of syndicate operations: *Hoodlum Empire* (1952)

tion. At one point Senator Stephens (Brian Donlevy) gives a speech concerning the 'innocent $2 bet' and its criminal consequences. In addition Nicolas Mancani (Luther Adler) gives a lengthy explanation to his nephew of his new 'business enterprise'. Pointing to a map of the United States prominently displayed on a wall, Mancani explains: 'What we don't own outright, we control outright!' In regard to the legitimacy of his newly formed syndicate, Mancani claims: 'Everybody wears a nice clean front ... I'm in real estate, Charlie's in oil, and Sporty there is an art dealer. ... Everybody's got something that's strictly legal.' The infiltration of organised crime into small-town America is depicted with Mancani's organisation establishing itself in Central City, where they attempt to place slot machines into a gas station owned and operated by Mancani's nephew, Joe Gray. Mancani again explains to his nephew, during a nighttime visit to his home, that the organisation is spreading out even into small towns. The octopus-like tentacles of organised crime, as it established a stranglehold across America, was a primary concern and a frequent metaphor of the Kevauver investigations. This conspiracy theory of organised crime was also a staple feature of a sub-genre of the syndicate film – the urban exposés of the mid-1950s, another Hollywood by-product of the Kefauver hearings.

The urban exposé crime thriller is associated with the transcontinental investigation of the Kefauver Committee by treating their narratives as true exposés of crime and corruption in their designated metropolitan settings. Many of the films were located in the same urban centres that the committee itself held hearings: *The Miami Story* (1955), *New York Confidential* (1955), *Chicago Syndicate* (1955), *New Orleans Uncensored* (1955), *Miami Exposé* (1956), *Inside Detroit* (1956), and *Chicago Confidential* (1957). Others exposed criminal activity in such locales as Texas (*The Houston Story* (1955)), Alabama (*The Phenix City Story* (1955)), and Oregon (*Portland Exposé* (1957)). Will Straw writes that 'most of these films claimed, in their opening sequences or in the posters which advertised them, some link to a real-life investigation of municipal vice and corruption' (1997: 111). In addition they almost always alluded to or emphasised the involvement of the syndicate in their respective locales, in keeping with the findings and conclusions of the Kefauver Committee. The template for the urban exposé sub-cycle, however, did not contain a real location within its title; instead it emphasised a key image that binds this group of films: 'the captive city'.

The Captive City (1952) was the first production of Aspen Pictures, an independent production company formed by Robert Wise and Mark Robson. Filmed entirely on location, Wise recalled: 'We made the film entirely on location in Reno [Nevada]. We used the newspaper there, the city hall, the street. There was no process – we hung cameras on cars – we didn't shoot a foot in the studio. ... Filming was completed in February 1952 and the film was released on 26 March 1952' (quoted in Thompson 1995: 57–8). Both Wise (who directed the film) and Robson had formerly worked at RKO studios as editors and directors for the Val Lewton unit. Their experience at RKO is apparent throughout the film, particularly in its technical aspect (it was photographed with a Hoge lens, which helped with the deep-focus shots that are prevalent) and the atmosphere of terror and paranoia maintained in the film. Wise's taut direction was rewarded with generally favourable reviews. *The Captive City* took a different narrative approach to the syndicate film, exposing the cancerous undergrowth of organized crime beneath the veneer of normalcy in a small American town.

The Captive City begins with Jim Austin (John Forsythe) and his wife, Marge (Joan Camden), driving through the countryside in the early morning hours. They are being pursued, but it is not clear by whom. They seek haven at the police station in the small town of Warren. While they await notification of a police escort to the state capitol, Austin uses a nearby tape recorder to relate the events that have transpired. In an extended flashback he reveals that he is a newspaper editor in the small town of Kennington. When a local private detective, Clyde Nelson, who is seemingly working on a harmless divorce case, contacts him things begin to change. Nelson wishes to expose the small town as a front for organised crime and, specifically, to expose one of Kennington's leading businessmen, Murray Sirak (Victor Sutherland), whose divorce case Nelson was investigating. After talking to Chief Gillete (Ray Teal) of the Kennington Police Department, Austin dismisses the detective's conspiratorial ideas. However, when Nelson is murdered, Austin takes up the investigation. Accompanied by his photographer, Phil Harding (Martin Milner), Austin learns that the syndicate is using Kennington for its wire service facilities. Nicolas Fabretti is the mob boss who visits the small town from time to time from his headquarters in Florida. Austin begins to receive pressure from various members of the community, including the police chief, to drop the investigation. He succeeds in uncovering the whole sordid business – the crime, filth, and corruption – with the blessing and help of local authorities. When his photographer is brutally beaten and Sirak's wife (Marjorie Crossland) is killed, Austin decides to take his findings to the Kefauver Senate Crime Commission hearings at the Capitol. After driving all night and evading the mysterious car with Florida plates that is pursuing them, the Austins finally receive an escort and at the end enter the hearing room to testify before the crime committee.

In keeping with the atmosphere of paranoia, the syndicate forces are never actually seen in the film. Their presence is alluded to by the 'car with Florida plates' or newspaper and teletype reports, or even the mere mention of the name of Dominic Fabretti. Only the front activities and those who are being used by the syndicate are actually seen. Chief Gillette, Sirak, and others are the common people who are acting as agents or fronts for Fabretti and the mob, whether they know it or not. Many of the advertisements for the film also alluded to the 'syndicate' as an unseen but very real presence. Most ads featured a gigantic silhouetted figure of a gangster carrying a machine gun in one hand, looming over a city skyline – and in his other hand, puppet-like strings leading to various sections of the city. As part of the advertising campaign the veracity of the film was noted as well as the personal endorsement of Senator Kefauver himself who provided a brief epilogue to the film. This epilogue helped mediate the fictional narrative with real-world events, and was something that became a staple feature for the many urban exposés that were to follow in the mid-1950s.

To reveal the vice and corruption hidden behind a community's 'normalcy' there is a mediator within the narrative space of the film. In *The Captive City* it is Jim Austin who, through his voice-over narration (via the technology of the tape-recorder), explicates the events of the film. In other urban exposés the voice-over is often a 'voice of God'-style narration, which was frequently used in semi-documentary films of the late 1940s such as *House on 92nd Street, T-Men* and *The Naked City* (all 1948). This style of narration can be found in *New York Confidential, Miami Story, Miami Exposé, Chicago Confidential, The Houston Story*, and *New Orleans Uncensored.* Some urban exposés add a prologue provided by a public figure. In *The Miami Story,* Florida senator George A. Smathers gives a prologue. *Miami Exposé* is introduced by Mayor Randy Christmas, who warns the audience, 'It could happen in your state', and in *The Phenix City Story* the prologue is given by the people of the city itself who are being interviewed by a news reporter. The authenticity of the urban exposé narrative also extends to its frequent use of on-location photography. Many of these films were shot in their respective locations, providing a travelogue not only to the well-known features of their locales but also to the 'guilty' ones. As Straw suggests, urban exposé narratives 'are secondary to their cataloguing of vice, and to the formal organization of these films as sequences of scenes in night-clubs, gambling dens and along neon-lit streets' (1997: 111).

Inspired by the event and findings of the Kefauver Crime Committee, syndicate films reinforced the consensus view that America was being targeted from within, as well as without, its geographical boundaries. According to Jack Shadoian these films identified a parallel discourse with the anti-communist crusaders in 1950s America:

> Crime, like communism, is against the American way of life. The evils of these poisonous systems are analogous. Americans must stick together and support whatever measures, however extreme or unsavory, that a courageous individual adopts to penetrate syndicate operations and hierarchies. ... Crime is corruption that

exacts from the public good a daily price. It must be annihilated at its source. (2003: 176)

Concurrent with the syndicate cycle as it developed in the 1950–52 period, was another crime variant – the anti-communist films. These films, which included *I Married a Communist* (1950), *I Was a Communist for the FBI* (1951), *The Whip Hand* (1951), and *Big Jim McClain* (1952), examined the supposed threat of communism in America. The substitution of communist for gangster was not an entirely Hollywood concept. In a speech delivered at Columbia University on 10 July 1951 entitled 'Crime in America and Its Effects on Foreign Relations' Estes Kefauver compared racketeering and organised crime to totalitarian governments. He stated this in terms that could equally be applied to communists:

> The racketeer and the gambler are parasites on the community and the nation. They perform no useful service; they produce nothing. We found, during the course of our investigation, that these parasites drain from our people billions of dollars a year, which otherwise might be diverted into useful enterprises – which, instead of producing cases for the relief rolls, would produce substantial citizens working each day as part of a great team, to keep this a substantial country. (1951: 656)

Kefauver's insistence on a 'substantial' citizenry and country emphasised the dichotomy of the constructed 'American' with that of foreign-born gangsters and communists. The syndicate films that were spawned during this period helped reinforce those beliefs.

The Retro-Gangster Cycle (1957–61): The Historicised Gangster

During the late 1950s a cycle of gangster films emerged which have been referred to as retro-gangster films and nostalgia gangster bio-pics. This group of predominantly low-budget films recreated the criminal exploits of several notorious Depression-era gangsters. The cycle was initiated with Don Siegel's *Baby Face Nelson* (1957) and included *Machine Gun Kelly* (1958), *The Bonnie Parker Story* (1958), *Al Capone* (1959), *Ma Barker's Killer Brood* (1960), *The Rise and Fall of Legs Diamond* (1960), *Pretty Boy Floyd*

(1961), *Portrait of a Mobster* (1961), *King of the Roaring 20's – The Story of Arnold Rothstein* (1961), and *Mad Dog Coll* (1962). The historical specificity of the retro-gangster cycle is important for several reasons. It revived a distilled version of the classical gangster narrative of the 1930s with its related iconography and ideological concerns. In addition, these films often depended on excessive violent action and somewhat caricatured depictions of primarily sociopathic gangster imagery in their exploitative narratives.

Though these films concern Prohibition- and Depression-era gangsters as their titular protagonists, they are by no means historical in setting or *mise-en-scène*. Rather, they exemplify their industrial context as low-budget exploitation films that were primarily intended for teenage drive-in audiences of the late 1950s. Peter Stanfield, in writing about this particular cycle, contends that despite their historical specificity as 'biopics' of notorious 1930s gangsters, the films 'display a marked interest in relating their exploits to contemporary topical concerns' (2010: 185). For Stanfield that topical concern was the 1950s obsession with juvenile delinquency, thereby relating the film's exploitation to delinquent youth as 'punk hoodlums'. The retro-gangster film cycle of the late 1950s primarily accomplished this contemporary relevance by dispensing with historical verisimilitude in regard to art direction and clothing. As Stanfield points out, with the exception of a couple of vintage automobiles, other indexical markers of the 1930s are rarely present. He further claims that this disjuncture is purposefully done to 'mark the films as topical – to be seen to be of the moment, producing a distinct form of dialogue between the "past" and the "present"' (2010: 196). The importance here is in the way this particular cycle of gangster films attempts to relate to a contemporaneous audience through its exploitation of the gangster's aberrant anti-social personality and the fascination with violent crime itself. In many ways the King Brothers' *Dillinger* can be viewed as a precursor to this cycle – it was simply not as relevant to teenage audiences of 1945.

Fran Mason notes, concerning this cycle of 'nostalgia bio-pics', that their gangster characterisations were noted for the quality of excess. The primary focus of these 'exploitative' films, geared as they were towards a teenage, drive-in theatre audience, is on action and violence as spectacle. Mason states that there is 'a logic of excess within the cycle as each film tries to top its predecessors by making its characters more excessive and ruthless' (2002: 122). Freed from the moorings of social context and commentary, the films in the retro-gangster cycle highlight the gangster's aberrant nature as a sociopath whose excessive violent behavior is a chief characteristic. Additionally, he claims that these films 'demystify their gangsters by both emphasizing the aberrance ... and stressing the anti-social behavior that follows' (ibid.). Coincidentally this emphasis on the spectacle of action and violence becomes the image of the gangster that network television would incorporate into its crime programming in the late 1950s.

The Untouchables (ABC, 1959–63): Gangster Television

Following a two-part pilot for CBS's *Westinghouse Desilu Playhouse*, broadcast on 20 and 27 April 1959, the series *The Untouchables* began its weekly run on ABC on 15 October. Airing on Thursday nights at 9:30 EST, the action series chronicled the exploits of Treasury Department agent Eliot Ness and his elite squad of 'Untouchables' as they fought organised crime during the Prohibition era. Quinn Martin, the series' executive pro-ducer, would go on to produce such ABC action adventure programs as *The Fugitive* (1963–67), *The F.B.I.* (1965–74), *The Invaders* (1967–68) and *The Streets of San Francisco* (1972–77). According to an advertisement in *TV Guide*, ABC promoted the premiere as a 'New Kind of Series'. Part of this 'newness' can be attributed to the way the series combined action-adventure elements within the historicised crime drama structure. Crime television series 'appropriated both the western's spectacle of adventure and the crime show's narrative structure of enigma and resolution, com-bining these with an accentuated emphasis on style and image' (Osgerby & Gough-Yates 2001: 7). This emphasis, in regard to *The Untouchables*, entailed an action-driven narrative that featured violence. The series' only recurring characters were Eliot Ness, played by Robert Stack, and his squad of special agents. Guest stars such as character actors Nehemiah Persoff, Bruce Gordon, Neville Brand, Jack Weston, J. Carrol Naish and others were introduced each week playing a variety of gangsters, hoodlums, and rack-eteers. The series format was similar to 1950s police procedurals with the exception of its one-hour length and its historical setting. Most 1950s tel-evision crime dramas such as *Dragnet* (1951–59), *Gangbusters* (1952), and *Treasury Men in Action* (1951–54) centred on the routine investigation of

Gangster film iconography and conventions come to television in the early 1960s:
The Untouchables (1959–63)

a crime with justice being delivered within the 26-minute duration of the programme. *The Untouchables* was above all an action-adventure series where investigative procedure became subservient to physical action.

Within its historical framework, the use of a pseudo-documentary style in *The Untouchables* promoted a sense of historic realism. This realistic tone was embellished through the use of a voice-over narrator – famed newspaper columnist, Walter Winchell. The narrative voice contributed to a historical background that produced a sense of documentary-style realism through its 'you were there' journalistic approach. Another important aspect of this historic realism was the fact that the series was based on a memoir written by Eliot Ness and Oscar Fraley published in 1957. The book itself figures prominently in the opening credit sequence, where it is surrounded by iconic crime-related images: a .38 revolver, a box of bullets, and a pair of handcuffs. This pseudo-documentary style was important in developing the narrative strategy of the series that relied not only on a historical framework but also on generic conventions associated with the gangster film.

The historical setting of Prohibition-era Chicago drew on the generic traits of the classic gangster cycle of the early 1930s. *The Untouchables* engaged its audience through the utilisation of generic codes associated with the gangster film that functioned as a form of cultural shorthand. Edward G. Robinson's tommy gun, haberdashery, and pin-striped suits from *Little Caesar* would be revived in Eliot Ness's battles with organised crime. By combining elements of the police drama with the gangster film and placing it within the context of the American 1930s, *The Untouchables* became not only a popular programme but also a controversial one. An understanding of *The Untouchables* and the controversy that surrounded the series necessitates an understanding of its generic elements and how those elements were received and responded to by its audience.

The Untouchables engaged its television audience immediately through violent physical action via the pre-credit 'teaser' sequence that showcased a scene of violence within the episode. Rather than initiating the narrative action, the teaser sequence was repeated within the episode itself as part of the narrative action. Functioning as an enticement for television viewers in the 1960s the industrial strategy emphasized the most distinguishing, albeit notorious, aspect of the crime series – its violence. For example, the teaser for 'The White Slavers' (3/10/60) consists of a gun battle between Ness's men and a number of gangsters. Similarly, 'The Tr-State Gang' (12/10/59) opens with Eliot Ness gunning down a gangster attempting to flee on a fire escape. In 'The Purple Gang' (12/01/60) a kidnap victim is shot as his wife pleads over the telephone for more time to come up with the ransom money. The teaser sequence promised viewers that violent gangster-style action was to follow and distinguished this television crime series from others, thereby insuring its popular success.

The ratings success of the series delivered ABC to the top position (35.1 Arbitron ranking) among the three US television networks (along with NBC and CBS) in 1960. Until this time ABC, according to Eric Barnouw, had always been referred to as the 'also ran network'; 'this third-place position was due to its late arrival in broadcasting history' (1977: 261). And it was the popularity of *The Untouchables* that stimulated a firestorm of political debate that began in 1961 about depictions of violence and crime on television and its effect on children.

On 15 October 1959 ABC broadcast the much anticipated debut of *The Untouchables* with an episode entitled 'The Empty Chair'. The very first image that the viewer encountered was the machine-gun slaying of two gangsters in a barbershop by Frank Nitti (Bruce Gordon). The violent action introduced on television screens within seconds of the opening sequence captured the attention of audiences and critics alike. The violence associated with *The Untouchables* was also a reflection of ABC-TV's attempts to 'muscle in' on the competing networks through more action-oriented programming. According to some historians and critics ABC-TV, through such programming strategies, helped kill off the 'Golden Age of Television' in the process. The 1953 merger of ABC with United Paramount Theatres (UPT) helped the fledgling network break the duopoly of CBS and NBC in broadcast television. That merger also signalled what would become ABC-TV's major focus – the emphasis on film programming (most of which would be produced on the West Coast), rather than live broadcasts. Prior to 1953 the majority of ABC-TV's programming output was similar to the other networks, consisting of game shows, news, sports programming, and a few sitcoms; ABC hardly stood out as a contender in early 1950s television broadcasting. The shift to filmed episodic series, rather than specialised live television, created an alternative programming form that, according to historian Christopher Anderson, 'encouraged an experience of television viewing as something ordinary, one component of the family's household routine' (1994: 12). ABC-TV's emphasis on action-adventure genre programming allowed for its continued reliance on telefilm producers from both the independents and major studios. The ratings success of both *Disneyland* and *Cheyenne* during the 1954–55 season prompted ABC to emphasise genre programming in part to differentiate its product. With the premiere of *The Untouchables* during the 1959–60 television season, ABC decided to place it in its Thursday night late prime-time schedule against the dramatic anthology series, *Playhouse 90* (CBS, 1956–60). The appeal of the Prohibition-era gangster series in large urban markets, where the dramatic anthology series had previously maintained a cultural appeal, doomed *Playhouse 90,* which was cancelled in 1960.

The basic narrative pattern for *The Untouchables* helped to ensure its success. By beginning with a violent pre-credit action sequence, the programme would immediately catch the attention and emotional response of the viewer. The pre-credit sequence serves the same purpose as a movie trailer – giving the potential viewer a preview of what to expect if they watch the episode. Following the opening credits, Walter Winchell's narrative voice provided a documentary-styled mediation that helps to negotiate the supposed historicity of characters and events with the action-adventure narrative. Winchell's typically rapid-fire, staccato vocal delivery created the illusion that the events unfolding are indeed true. The voice-over also served a narrative function by providing necessary expository material that in turn allows for more physical action within the programme. This function 'allows filmmakers to traverse continents or decades without fear of leaving the viewer behind. The overt presence of the narrator, who speaks from a privileged vantage point and knits together all of the loose threads, allows for any number of shifts of focalization without strain' (Kozloff 1988: 80).

The narrative pattern that follows the opening credits alternates scenes between gangsters and Eliot Ness's squad of prohibition agents. That the episodes typically open with a scene focusing on the gangsters privileges these characters as the real narrative focus of the programme. The titles of individual episodes also illustrates this preferential treatment for the gangster as the central character: 'Ma Barker and Her Boys', 'The Dutch Schultz Story', 'The Frank Nitti Story', 'The Genna Brothers', 'The Waxey Gordon Story', 'Jack "Legs" Diamond', 'The Purple Gang', 'The Tri-State Gang' and so on. This subversive narrative focus effectively places the recurring gangster characterisations such as Jake 'Greasy Thumb' Guzak, Joe Kulak, Louis 'Lepke' Buchalter, and, especially, Frank Nitti as the real 'stars' of the series. And it is the public's fascination with the gangster and the forcefulness of his presence that attracted the wide audience that enabled the popularity and notoriety of the series in the 1960s. A major part of that fascination is what Robert Warshow calls the 'quality of irrational brutality'. This unique feature of the gangster's image 'becomes at once the means to success and the content of success – a success that is defined in its most general terms, not as accomplishment or gain, but simply as the unlimited possibility of aggression' (1962: 132). The brutality, aggression, and sadism associated with the gangster's image, real and imaginary, and the regular appearance of that image on network television created a moral panic in the early 1960s concerning television violence.

The controversy *The Untouchables* echoes the same efforts by moral guardians of the early 1930s in regard to the gangster film. Many criticised the series for its depiction of brutal violence and its supposed historical framework. By combining the G-man narrative formula with its weekly parade of notorious gangsters of the 1930s, the series basically brought the conventions of the gangster film to the medium of television, and its violence and criminality with it. Though, as Tise Vahimagi notes, the series was 'not only exploitational, but colorfully theatrical' offering its viewers 'a peculiar history lesson represented in comic-book style' (1998: 2); it was widely regarded as being a 'true' depiction of events through its unique quasi-historical framing device. Because it was on network television during the antenna age it was widely disseminated to a mass audience, including children – much like its gangster film predecessors. Because of its dissemination across the mass media of network television in the early 1960s *The Untouchables* courted controversy because of its gangster conventions – in the contemporary media the niche marketing of series such as *Boardwalk Empire* with its even more gratuitous violence barely raises an eyebrow.

Notes

1   An addendum to the Production Code was added on 3 December 1947, Resolution No. 13, that read as follows: 'No picture shall be approved that deals with the life of a notorious criminal of current or recent times, that uses the name, nickname, or alias of such a notorious criminal in the film, nor shall a picture be approved if based on the life of such a notorious criminal unless the character shown in the film be punished for crimes shown in the film as committed by him', cited in Thomas Doherty (2007) *Hollywood's Censor: Joseph I. Breen & The Production Code Administration*. New York: Columbia University Press, 356.

2   For more information concerning the Kefauver Hearings see Lee Bernstein (2002) *The Greatest Menace: Organized Crime in Cold War America*. Amherst, MA: University of Massachusetts Press.

4 LA FAMIGLIA: COPPOLA, SCORSESE, AND GANGSTER ETHNICITY

> Leave the gun, take the canolli.
>
> Clemenza in *The Godfather* (1972)

The above quotation is one of perhaps a half dozen lines from Francis Ford Coppola's film that are immediately recognizable and oft-quoted in popular culture around the world. Significantly, it connects gangster culture with Italian ethnicity in a landmark film emphasizing that ethnicity as its central thematic core. This linkage between criminality and Italian heritage has become associated with the gangster film genre from its origins to the present day. A study conducted from 1996 to 2002 on Italian culture on film (1928–2002) found that of the 1,233 Italian-related films made since the sound era (circa 1928) 69% portrayed Italians in a negative light. Out of this same number of films, 500 (40%) dealt with mob characters either as authentic characters (12%) or fictionalized characters (88%). Another statistic from the same study indicates the influence of *The Godfather* by claiming that close to 300 movies featuring Italians as criminals were produced since the success of the film, an average of nine films a year from 1972 to 2002.[1] These statistics indicate not only a bias concerning Italian stereotypes in gangster films but that a standard barometer for these depictions is one film in particular – *The Godfather*. This film basically changed the representation of the gangster in American cinema and refocused gangster imagery to the portrayal of a sympathetic criminal and his cultural values. These stereotypical images are not new and can be dated to the very origins of the film genre itself, as well as other media sources. Yet the idea of mob-related ethnicity, particularly the idea of Italianicity, becomes more pronounced in the 1970s with the work of two Italian-American filmmakers, Francis Ford Coppola and Martin Scorsese.

Both directors were part of the New Hollywood cinema of the 1970s and were able to express their Italian-American background and cultural herit-age through their gangster-related films. For Coppola there was a historical, grandiose depiction of the epic story of the Corleones in America; whereas Scorsese focused on the 'mean streets' of contemporary urban life and the hoodlums, gangsters, and wise guys that populated them. Both directors are endemic to the development of the contemporary American gangster film in terms of historicity and ethnic representation. As Peter Bondanella suggests in relation to both directors' gangster films, 'to ignore the inter-textual links between all these works [he also includes David Chase's HBO series *The Sopranos*] would be something similar to evaluating the place of the Civil War in American popular culture without taking into account the impact of *Gone With the Wind*' (2004: 271). The sweeping historical epic style of Coppola and the smaller, more personal style of Scorsese provide a framework for directors such as Sergio Leone (*Once Upon a Time in America* (1984)), John Huston (*Prizzi's Honor* (1985)), Joel Cohen (*Miller's Crossing* (1990)), Robert de Niro (*A Bronx Tale* (1993)) and Mike Newell (*Donnie Brasco* (1997)) to follow in presenting crime-related narratives and ethnicity on screen.

The post-classical gangster film is noted for its urban realism and graphic violence. Carlos Cortes has distinguished this period from 1970 to 1988 as an era of ethnic commercialization that 'reflected general trends in US society, including filmmaking' (1987: 116). The ethnic revival during the 1960s and 1970s championed civil rights and social justice, but was also a celebration of ethnic heritage. He further notes that Hollywood saw the commercial possibilities of ethnicity that gave rise to the production of ethnic-themed films, including Italian-American-themed films, that were primarily crime films. The scrapping of the Hays Production Code and the subsequent implementation of a ratings system by the MPPDA in 1968 also bolstered this boom in ethnic-related content on screen. Following the formation of the PCA in 1934 and the enforcement of the Production Code through the auspices of its administrator Joseph Breen, ethnic representation was erased or censured on American screens. As Jonathan Munby argues, part of the need for Code enforcement addressed the 'hyphenated identity' of the ethnic gangster and the threat to the WASP 'normative' status; the popular appeal of gangster films of the early 1930s created a 'national identification with an ethnic urban type' (1999: 44). After 1934 the gangster became associated with either the American outlaw type or a homogenised racketeer void of any ethnic markings. In the post-war era this erasure continued though there were sporadic films (to be discussed in the following section) that created a demonisation of ethnicity as 'other', yet these did not constitute a production cycle.[2] In fact many of these films reverted to negative stereotypes of the early silent era. By contrast, the New Hollywood filmmakers were now able to address ethnicity head on thereby adding a certain amount of realism to their hyphenated identity through the use of cultural values as well as ethnic heritage.

In addition to ethnicity, graphic violence was also depicted more realistically on screen in New Hollywood cinema. Beginning with Arthur Penn (*Bonnie and Clyde*) and Sam Peckinpah (*The Wild Bunch*), filmmakers were able to 'combine graphic violence with thematic complexity, proving that visceral onscreen bloodshed could be used seriously, not just for exploitation' (Kendrick 2009: 102). This was not an issue of violence for violence's sake, but neither was it a coded reference (through either shadow play or suggestive violence) to the portrayal of violence that was required in the stipulations of the Production Code. It is difficult to conceive of either the brutal shooting of Sonny Corleone (James Caan) in *The Godfather* or the violent sadism associated with Tommy Devito (Joe Pesci) in *Goodfellas* without the use of graphic violence as a cinematic narrative tool for the filmmakers to utilize in an effective manner. This addition of visual realism to the filmmaker's palette was accompanied by an urban street realism that often emphasized ethnicity. It was an ethnic realism unlike its cinematic forbearers in depicting a secretive criminal organization that became exacerbated through the work of two filmmakers in particular.

Early Mafia Films

A distinguishing characteristic of early screen representations of the Mafia is that they focused almost entirely on the depiction of a particular crime and criminality with few indications of cultural identity or heritage. Many of these early films centered on a local criminal gang phenomena known as 'The Black Hand', a loosely organized group of extortionists that preyed primarily on Italian immigrant communities in metropolitan areas of turn-of-the-century America.[3] Eventually, the Black Hand became synonymous with the Mafia in American films; it is even directly referenced through the character of the local Black Hand, Don Fanucci (Gaston Moschin), in *The Godfather, Part II* (1974). Fanucci is a localized criminal who still maintains some respect and notoriety in the Italian community through his threats of violence and his commanding, albeit melodramatic, presence. Early screen portrayals of the Black Hand centered on authentic newspaper accounts of their extortion activities that involved kidnapping, mutilation, and arson. These activities provided the film's narrative structure that frequently hinged on revenge or cops-and-robbers dramatic formulas.

Wallace McCutcheon's *The Black Hand* (1906), recently restored by the Library of Congress, is considered the first Mafia movie and concerns a real-life kidnapping attempt by a small gang that had occurred several weeks (February 1906) prior to the film's production and release (March 1906). Vicenzo Maggitti considers the film the Mafia genre's ur-text through its depiction of a Black Hand-style crime and its visual representation of a topical event. According to Maggitti, 'these films attempted to reflect the reality of the Italian immigrants' experiences in the United States, one in which victims and gangsters were likely to share the same neighborhood and often place of origin (the western area of Sicily)' (2011: 52). The one-reel film was based on a newspaper account of the actual Black Hand kidnapping of a storekeeper's daughter, and the apprehension of the criminals by the New York police. The original title of the film – *The Black Hand: True Story of a Recent Occurrence in the Italian Quarter of New York* – also addresses its topicality for contemporary audiences and it was produced and released within weeks of the actual crime itself. Maggitti suggests that the film served a pedagogical purpose as well by showing that 'social ills were exacerbated by the rising tide of immigrants, whose lifestyle seemed to include criminality as one of its main cultural components' (2011: 51). Therefore the film can be viewed as a social issue document relevant to turn-of-the-century urban ethnic audiences. The film follows a crime-and-apprehension approach where the planning of the crime is depicted, followed by the kidnapping of the victim, and finally the apprehension of the criminals by the police. Much like *Musketeers of*

Pig Alley the exterior sequence of the kidnapping itself is shot outdoors in the snow-covered streets of New York City. The films' importance lies in its topicality to recent events and its depiction of a secretive criminal conspiracy that preyed on Italian immigrants. The Black Hand connection to turn-of-the-century America creates a specific historical framework that will be followed in subsequent films.

Richard Thorpe's *Black Hand* (1950) also concerns the nefarious criminal organization and is likewise partially based on a true incident – the killing of New York Police detective, Joseph Petrosino of the 'Italian Squad' in Palermo, Sicily on 12 March 1909, shortly after arriving to investigate Mafia connections to Black Hand activity in New York City. This incident had been treated in silent films, most notably in *The Adventures of Lieutenant Petrosino* (Feature Photoplay Co., 1912). Thorpe's film was an MGM production starring Gene Kelley in his first dramatic role as a young lawyer seeking to avenge the killing of his father years earlier by the Black Hand. Marc Lawrence plays the Black Hand Mafioso, Caesar Xavier Serpi and J. Carroll Naish portrays police detective, Louis Lorelli (patterned after Petrosino) who is assassinated by Serpi's agents in Sicily while investigating Black Hand activities. The film also depicts a clandestine criminal group and the attempts to bring it to justice. In 1959 director Richard Wilson focused entirely on the career of Lieutenant Petrosino in *Pay or Die!* (Allied Artists, 1959) starring Ernest Borgnine as the ill-fated police detective.

These films presented a historicized version of early Mafia activities within a cops-and-robbers or revenge-type narrative structure. In these films the representatives of the Black Hand are portrayed as foreign-born criminals (typically Sicilian) who victimize Italian immigrants through extortion practices, including violence. Altogether the Black Hand films showcase 'an interest in the historical origins of Italian American criminality as well as the reconstruction of the Little Italies at the beginning of the twentieth century that produced such criminals' (Bondanella 2004: 223). With the exception of a low-budget, topical potboiler by director Edward L. Cahn entitled *Inside the Mafia* (1959), few Hollywood films of the studio era dealt with the subject of the contemporary Mafia. Once again topical events concerning organized crime, and the Mafia in particular, were to influence the further development of the American gangster film. The Valachi Hearings of 1963 exposed the existence of 'La Cosa Nostra' and its Old World traditions to the American public. Joseph Valachi, a former soldier in the Genovese crime family, testified before Senator John L. McClellan's Subcommittee on Investigations on Government Operations, informing them of clandestine Mafia operations and rituals. The Valachi testimony created an increased public awareness of the secretive criminal society that would soon become a part of popular culture.

Martin Ritt's *The Brotherhood* (1968), released by Paramount Pictures, represents a distinct cultural shift in representations of the mafia on film. According to Robert Casillo, the film is often regarded as 'the closest cinematic adumbration of *The Godfather*' through its 'exploration of Mafia familism, tradition, social codes, and Old World origins' (2011: 85). A key characteristic of this shift is that Mafia representation moves from an aberrant image based on a criminal 'other' to a normative one based on family alliances and values. *The Brotherhood* showcases a film narrative that is completely immersed in mafia culture. There is no law enforcement restoration of societal order narrative structure in the film, by contrast it is centered (as is *The Godfather*) on a particular family and the internal conflicts between family (both familial and crime) members. The film revolves around the Ginetta brothers, Frank (Kirk Douglas) and Vince (Alex Cord), and their contested relationship with their criminal syndicate. Frank, the elder brother, represents 'Old School' Mafia culture steeped in Sicilian traditional values. Whereas Vince, the younger, is more representative of modern contemporary values and change. The two brothers clash when the syndicate, referred to in the film as 'The Board', want to expand into electronics in order to infiltrate government industries through military and space programs. Frank is opposed to the idea knowing that the government itself would never allow it to happen, whereas Vince sees this as a sign of progress effectively moving the syndicate into the modern world. Frank's 'Old World' vendetta style ultimately gets him into trouble with the Board when he kills a member of the organization, his brother's father-in-law, Dominick Bertoldo (Luther Adler), to avenge the death of his father and forty other Mafioso during the formation of the modern syndicate under Charles 'Lucky' Luciano. Forced into exile in Sicily because of the execution, Frank allows for his own assassination at the hand of his brother Vince in traditional Sicilian fashion.

The film continually references the dichotomy between traditional culture and mores and modern corporate society through visual means. In the opening pre-credit sequence Vince boards an airliner bound for

Sicily. The conveniences of modern travel are juxtaposed with the rugged Sicilian landscape once he arrives in Palermo, with modernity also present in the Old World via motorcycles and telephones. Yet the Old World is still very much present in the language and the customs of the people. This dichotomy of values is also illustrated by the extensive use of on-location photography in the film as it shifts between the skyscraper-laden vertically man-made skylines of New York City to the rustic pastoral landscape of Sicily. According to Casillo, Kirk Douglas (who also served as the film's producer) insisted on shooting on location in New York and Sicily, rather than use sound stages (2011: 86). The use of location cinematography enhances the juxtaposition of the old world and the new world in the film and the contrast between traditionalism and modernism. This dichotomy is also exemplified in the appearance of the Ginetta brothers themselves. Frank is heavily mustached, thereby representing the old-style patriarchal 'Mustache Petes' of traditional Mafia families. He is often seen associating with his late father's older friends (also heavily mustached) by speaking Sicilian, drinking, attending funerals, and playing bocce ball, a traditional Italian outdoor game. Frank is also more of an extrovert, often playing practical jokes and has a penchant for sarcasm. When told at a meeting of the Board that they should suppress their personalities and become more like 'the wallpaper, like the furniture'. Frank mockingly replies: 'Okay, I'm a chair.' By contrast, Vince has a clean-shaven appearance and is often seen working at his desk or conferring and agreeing with the modern corporate syndicate ideas of the Board. He seldom speaks in Sicilian and 'embodies the second-generation Italian-American male hungry for assimilation at virtually any cost' (Casillo 2011: 89).

Sicilian culture is present throughout the film that begins with a wedding celebration and ends with equally festive outdoor feasting and drinking prior to Frank's assassination. Traditional songs and music are also utilized throughout the film to suggest the continued presence of Mafia culture even in modern America. Perhaps the most representative example of Mafia culture in the film is its depictions of vendetta-style justice by violence. As part of the extended flashback sequence at the beginning of the film Frank has an informant killed and a dead canary placed in the corpse's mouth – a sign of the Sicilian justice for those who 'sing'. Frank himself personally presides over the execution of Bertoldo, the mob boss responsible for submitting the names of the '41' who were murdered under

Luciano's orders. Bertoldo is hog-tied with a rope and as a result is slowly strangled as he vainly struggles to free himself. While this occurs Frank methodically pronounces the individual names of the '41' in his presence. The final act of violence in the film occurs when Frank gives Vince their father's shotgun in order to perform the 'hit' that he was ordered to do by the Board. Each violent act illustrates the traditional Mafia-style vendetta action that is considered old-style justice and is part of the film's primary theme concerning familial conflict and business, a theme that will also be a central concern of *The Godfather* trilogy.

The Cultural Significance of The Godfather

Tom Santopietro's *The Godfather Effect* (2012) argues that the initial film in the trilogy succeeded in defining what it means to be an American, whether or not you are Italian. The cultural effects of Coppola's saga of the Corleone family rendered Italianness as a global phenomena through its depiction of a crime family and its dissolution over time. As Santopietro states:

> With this one film, notions of ethnicity in America had been upended in a rather spectacular fashion. Mobsters these characters may have been, but in their proud self-assertion, celebration of ethnicity, and love of family lay complex, readily identifiable human beings. For the very first time, Italian-Americans were not just embracing their own story but telling it in their own terms. (2012: 6)

The idea of a proud ethnicity is an important part of the film's success, as it indicates a respect for the characters and the narrative, as well as the cultural heritage that frames the story itself. *The Godfather*, even more so than its predecessor, *The Brotherhood*, was distinguished by the cultural centrality on family and business – the one reflecting Sicilian values and the other the American Dream of individual success. It is also important that the filmmaker, screenwriter, crew, and many cast members were Italian-Americans; this inflects the film with what Vera Dika refers to as 'Italianicity', cultural codes throughout the trilogy that render the notion of 'Italianness' (2000: 77). In this sense, Coppola's trilogy represents a meditation on the quest for both individual and national identity through the lives of the Corleone family.

The idea of family is central to Italian culture and is also most important to the Mafioso; because it references a dualism – the blood family and the Mafia family. The opening lines of the film, 'I believe in America', spoken by the undertaker Amerigo Bonasera during his visit with Don Corleone is his prelude to the account of his daughter's violation at the hands of thugs and his quest for justice. The conventional avenue of American justice has failed, indicating that his dream of America has failed, so he comes to the Mafioso, Don Corleone, for vendetta-style justice. Yet since he is not a part of the Don's extended Mafia family through the tradition of friendship and service, the Don hesitates. Bonasera submissively requests that the Don be his friend and bowing to kiss his hand enacts a ritual of kinship that is key to understanding the patriarchal authority of the Mafioso beyond the kinship of blood relatives.

The concept of *la famiglia* is important in regard to the Mafioso because it marks a distinct shift away from previous images in gangster cinema. Earlier representations of the gangster as either racketeer or outlaw emphasized his individualism, his struggle to achieve success on his own terms and for himself. The gangster is often contrasted with normative society as an outsider who is, quite literally, attempting to force himself into that society. This is the thesis for Robert Warshow's seminal essay in describing the gangster as a tragic hero in American film. However, with regard to the Mafioso, there is a communal aspect to the idea of family that marks a symbiotic relationship between him and others. The Mafioso is connected to his cultural environment through his family and his heritage; it is a socialized structure that is ambivalent to individual enterprise. As Alessandro Camon notes:

> A Mafioso who works for himself is a theoretical impossibility, a flagrant violation of the organization's ethics. He needs a family to provide for, children to carry his name. The whole group of fellow Mafioso he is associated with is also called 'a family,' whose collective interest is inseparable from that of the individuals. This is the idea of the proletariat or of the aristocracy. It is not as deeply ingrained in the bourgeoisie. (2000: 60)

Similarly, John Paul Russo compares the thematic desire for plenitude represented by the family in the *Godfather* films to the classic social distinction between *Gemeinschaft*, a small clan or community based on social ties and vertical hierarchy, and *Gesellschaft*, an impersonal civil society formed by contractual bonds based on the attainment of particular ends (2011: 111). This social class distinction is important because it illustrates one of the basic conflicts in the trilogy: the tension between family and business that is personified in the character of Michael Corleone. It is a distinction that is also a central concern in viewing the films as a critique of the American Dream, in that this desire for success is based on a capitalist system that is based on material and not familial wealth. It is an individual enterprise rather than a communal one. This thematic tension between family and business reflects the basic conflict in the trilogy between Old World values and New World interests that is conceptualized by the immigrant experience in America.

Coppola's trilogy envisions the immigrant experience of assimilation through the contrast and eventual loss of Old World values with New World ideas. Significantly, the first film begins with a traditional wedding ceremony that signifies both the expansion of the family and the separation of one of its members, Vito's daughter, Connie. Communal ceremonies are present throughout the series of films – the baptism of Michael and Kay's son, Anthony, Don Vito's funeral, and Anthony's First Communion. These ceremonies mark a communal event that brings not only the birth family together but also the Mafia families. Traditional music, dancing, food, and drink mark many of these ceremonies. This Old World traditionalism that venerates the past is contrasted by the modernist values representative of New World culture that venerate the present and the possibility of the future. This New World culture gradually becomes more manifest throughout the films as Michael becomes assimilated into it and as a consequence loses his traditional Old World connections. This loss of Old World innocence, so to speak, is best exemplified through his progression in all three films – from a very real innocent, who has had nothing to do with the family business to exiled criminal, to Godfather, to CEO and world leader. As Camon notes, 'Michael Corleone, a man who had not chosen crime but was pulled into it to save the family's honor, struggles his whole life to achieve one goal: to become legitimate. He wants to take his immigrant family to the other side of the road' (2000: 66). In so doing, Michael's real loss of innocence is the loss of his Old World cultural roots in his desire for legitimacy in the new one.

The dichotomy between Old World and New World values is also addressed in the films representation of business ethics. The community service entrepreneurship of Vito Corleone, who initially provides a service to the Little Italy community by killing the Black Hand extortionist Don Fanucci, initially establishes a localised protection racket that gradually expands into other criminal activities. Business is conducted in the home, thereby equating it with family. In the first film, as Vito's daughter's wedding reception is taking place outside the family home, Vito is meeting with friends and acquaintances (clients) to provide favors (in return for their allegiance to the Mafia family). The family home as the center of both family and business is physically lost when Michael relocates from New York to Las Vegas in order to expand and closely supervise his business interests. This dislocation illustrates Michael's assimilation and loss of innocence by gradually breaking family ties and traditions associated with his father, Vito Corleone. In *The Godfather, Part III* (1990), Michael attempts to further legitimise himself and his now dysfunctional family by corporatising his business interest into the International Immobiliare, the world's largest real-estate company. The Corleone's global corporate empire represents the dissolution of his family business through his assimilation into the New World culture of materialism and individual wealth. His corporate interests belie the words that he utters in that last film: 'the only wealth in this world is children, more than all the money and power on Earth'. His quest for New World and global legitimization has distanced him from his family and his cultural heritage.

Francis Ford Coppola readily admitted during an interview in 1972 that his film offered a metaphoric vision:

> I always wanted to use the Mafia as a metaphor for America. If you look at the film you see that it is focused that way. ... I feel that the Mafia is an incredible metaphor for this country. Both are totally capitalistic phenomena and basically have a profit motive. (Quoted in Bondanella 2004: 239–40)

The rise and fall of the Corleone family from their immigrant status to leadership in global politics through the character of Michael Corleone charts an epic example of American capitalist endeavor and the subsequent loss of self. Though it is easily illustrated through the development of a criminal business empire it is also indicated visually in the film's striking *mise-en-scène* composition. Three images in particular provide examples of Coppola's critique of the American Dream. The first is the opening wedding scene itself. While the festivities are taking place outdoors in the abundant sunshine of the Corleone estate, inside the home in the darkly-lit interior office of the Mafioso, Don Vito is rewarding his supplicants with gifts of service as gratitude for their allegiance to his family. Gordon Willis (often called the 'Prince of Darkness' for his fondness for low lighting levels) effectively used chiaroscuro photography to perfectly display the clandestine world of the Mafioso that operates, literally, behind closed doors. It is a private world that captures the hidden organization of justice that renders American justice through courts and corruption moot. In essence, the operations of the Don showcase the puppet-like machinations of the Mafia through secrecy and subterfuge, thereby destroying the illusion of the Puritan ethic of success through hard work and perseverance. Though the metaphor for capitalism becomes much more pronounced through the character of Michael Corleone, it begins here as an illustration of the nature of the way the Mafia has infiltrated American society.

On a different visual level the metaphor is presented ironically through the use of the penultimate American icon of immigrant freedom – the Statue of Liberty. After the unsuccessful assassination attempt on Don Vito by Sollazzo 'the Turk', Sonny Corleone orders Paulie Gatto, the Don's driver, hit because he suspects him of being a traitor and informant to Sollazzo. Clemenza and Lampone have Paulie drive them throughout New York on various odd jobs. When they are driving through the countryside near Ellis Island, Clemenza orders Paulie to stop the car so that he can relieve himself. Coppola frames the killing of Paulie in a long shot that shows the car with Paulie behind the wheel, Lampone's hand holding a gun comes into the shot and we hear three shots as the edit returns to Clemenza. Throughout the composition of Paulie's hit the Statue of Liberty is seen in the distance in the far left horizon of the frame. The icon is distant yet clearly visible to the viewer, seated within a sea of wind-blown tall grass. The irony of Amerigo Bonasera's opening words, 'I believe in America', seem to re-echo through the visual image alone. The visual metaphor is significantly ironic for the viewer as it implies on a metaphoric level the denial of freedom to those unfortunate to become a traitor to the Mafia family. It is also the first instance of how the Corleone family

Young Vito Corleone arrives at the land of opportunity: *The Godfather, Part II* (1974)

conducts 'business' by protecting their family and their interests through violent vendetta-style justice. Likewise, it is significant that we see the back of the Statue of Liberty in the composition, as if it were turning away from the criminal activities of its immigrant children.

An even more striking example of the metaphoric use of the Statue of Liberty occurs in *The Godfather, Part II*, when the young Vito Andolini (later christened 'Corleone' by an impatient Ellis Island official) arrives to the United States. As the ship carrying Vito pulls into the harbor we see him amid a crowd of other immigrants looking vacantly at the welcoming statue, not knowing what to expect in the New World. The next scene is inside Ellis Island as the immigrants are herded like cattle for their authorization documents. Vito, quarantined because of suspected tuberculosis and separated from the others, is confined in a prison-like cell. Outside his window is the Statue of Liberty that is initially seen in reflection on the window itself next to Vito Corleone. The image has now been given again an ironic quality through the circumstance of Vito's confinement and the supposed promise of freedom in the New World. This irony is strengthened by the song that Vito Corleone begins to softly sing as he looks out the window towards the Statue of Liberty. It is a Sicilian folk song called '*Lu Sciccareddu*' ('The Donkey') and Vito sings the first verse of the song:

Avia 'nu sciccareddu, ma veru sapuritu.
A mia mi l'amazzaru, poveru sceccu miu

[I had a little donkey, truly cute (or funny).
They have killed it, poor little donkey of mine.]

The lyrics suggest the loss of something dear and the ironic implication
to the song is that Vito, too, has suffered a loss – the loss of family in
Sicily, where is brother and mother were killed by vendetta, and his loss of
innocence. As the rest of the film attests, Vito Corleone begins afresh in the
New World, and builds a family and a business in the process of becoming
an American.

The importance of *The Godfather* trilogy to the American gangster film
lies in its ability to revitalize the genre through its historical scope, its rec-
lamation of the sympathetic gangster as the central character, and its total
immersion into a cultural heritage that emphasizes family traditions and
values. It is no coincidence that when Francis Ford Coppola re-edited *The
Godfather* and *The Godfather, Part II* for broadcast television in 1977 as *The
Godfather Saga: A Novel for Television*, he did so by placing it in chronological order. Alex Haley's *Roots* aired earlier that same year, and Coppola's
films fit perfectly into the historicized epic format and the cultural/ethnic
heritage narrative of the television mini-series. While *The Godfather* films
present an epic romanticized version of the Mafia and the gangster film,
another Italian-American film director, Martin Scorsese, brought the gangster genre back to its social environmental roots of the urban mean streets
and its wise guy inhabitants. If Coppola primarily focuses on the Corleone
family as representative of the hierarchical structure of the Mafia, Scorsese
pays more attention to the families' workers, the soldiers of the Don (such
as Clemenza, Tessio, and Paulie) and their individual personalities and
struggles.

Martin Scorsese and Street Values

Martin Scorsese is significant to the post-classical development of the
gangster film primarily because he focuses on the daily minutiae of mob
life. Scorsese's background of growing up in New York's Little Italy environment provided him with the ability to both participate and observe life on

the streets and it is this participatory-observational approach to filmmaking that created a different perspective to the gangster film genre. In his assessment of *Mean Streets* (1973), film historian Carlos Clarens remarked that Scorsese's gangsters 'would hardly think of themselves as criminals … they are stunted adolescents bound together by endless wheeling and dealing, boozing and whoring, and the boundaries of a turf they defend jealously against outsiders' (1980: 325). This documentation of a hedonistic lifestyle that is comprised of temporary actions and momentary pleasures is a seminal characteristic of Scorsese's gangster films. He simply records their activities as if he were an ethnographer documenting a particular case study. Scorsese himself once stated that, in regard to *Mean Streets*, 'it was an attempt to put myself and my old friends on the screen, to show how we lived, what life was like in Little Italy. It was really an anthropological or a sociological tract' (quoted in Christie & Thompson 2003: 48). This type of documentary quality can also be observed in the other films that make up what Robert Casillo describes as Scorsese's 'wise guy trilogy': *Goodfellas* and *Casino* (1995). Certain stylistic devices that are characteristic of documentary filmmaking mark this filmmaking quality: the use of voice-over narration, the sporadic use of inter-titles describing place and time, location cinematography, and the frequent use of hand-held or mobile camera movements. This produces an aspect of urban realism that creates an observational awareness in the viewer that at the same time allows a certain amount of participation in the characters and their actions.

An example of this documentary-like approach can be found in a short film that Scorsese made in 1974, *Italianamerican*; although it is not a gangster film, it is central to an understanding of the type of approach the director will take in his 'wise guy trilogy' and some of his other films. As one critic once observed, *Italianamerican* represents 'the bedrock of Scorsese's art' (Casillo 2007: 36). The early work of Scorsese is best viewed as part of the ethnic revival of the 1970s with its fascination towards cultural awareness. As a third-generation Italian-American, Scorsese focused much of his personal filmmaking on recording the experiences of street life and recounting the cultural heritage of Little Italy. The roots of all of Scorsese's gangster films from *Mean Streets* to *The Departed* (2006) lie in this awareness of one's history and culture and its relationship to place. *Italianamerican* is specifically located in the Scorsese family apartment on

Elizabeth Street, where during the course of the 49-minute documentary, Catherine Scorsese, Martin's mother, prepares pasta sauce while conversation and queries (by a primarily off-screen Martin) provides an insight into the family itself. Made for the American Bicentennial Celebration, the 'gravy' that Scorsese's mother cooks is emblematic of the 'hybridity of Italian America itself' (Casillo 2007: 55) through its combination of canned and fresh ingredients, the preparation of the meatballs for the sauce – the mixture of food essentially becomes a metaphor for the melting pot of American culture. Like his gangster films, the documentary evinces a realistic approach to its subject and the revelatory nature of the minutiae of everyday life. Food preparation becomes a communal act that is both ritualistic and satisfying. Visually the films confined *mise-en-scène*, especially when the viewer enters the maternal domain of the kitchen, is revelatory because 'it is as if we were entering the family's inner sanctum, its secret core of power, the ultimate source of its providence' (Casillo 2007: 54). This becomes a key element in many Scorsese films, especially through his fondness for long tracking shots that are equally revelatory – Tony's bar and the restaurant owned by Uncle Giovanni (the local Mafioso) in *Mean Streets*, the Bamboo Lounge in *Goodfellas*, and the Tangiers in *Casino*. These eatery and pleasure establishments represent the gradual displacement and assimilation of Italian-Americans into American culture and essentially become surrogate domestic kitchens turned into businesses. This displacement is registered visually through Scorsese's use of the long mobile shot that physically moves the viewer and the characters through the space. The geographic displacement of the Italian-American gangster from Sicily to New York and New Jersey and to the far west of Las Vegas and beyond, and the cultural ramifications of this displacement, are a central motif in Scorsese's 'wise guy' trilogy.

Unlike Coppola's aristocratic Corleone family and the epic narrative structure of the family's dissolution over time, Scorsese concentrates on the low-level small-time hoods' struggle for survival on the streets and their attempts at material success. In this respect, Scorsese's gangsters are very much like Tommy Powers and Matt Doyle in William Wellman's *The Public Enemy*. Scorsese himself often recounted his seeing both *Little Caesar* and *The Public Enemy* on a double-bill in the 1950s. He stated that he 'felt *Little Caesar* to be vulgar, very overdone, and heavily acted. But even though they were Irish gangsters in *The Public Enemy* ... we understood the thinking behind it' (quoted in Christie & Thompson 2003: 45).[4] Much of that 'thinking' centers on the gangster's conspicuous consumption as a marker for success. The acquisition of material goods, rather than wealth and power, denotes the primary concern of wise guy 'street smart' philosophy. This materialist culture is displayed through clothes, cars, and women – particularly through the gangster's clothes. In *Goodfellas*, for instance, when a young adolescent Henry Hill displays his newly purchased (through the money he makes from the local mob) fashionable attire to his mother, her immediate verbal reaction is, 'My God! You look like a gangster!' Likewise, Charlie (Harvey Keitel) in *Mean Streets* is fashionably dressed in double-suited jackets and ties, especially when he is seen with his Uncle Giovanni, the local Mafioso. It is the seduction of gangster life that appeals to the Scorsese wise guys who bypass the traditional avenues of success through hard work by working for the mob as gofers, collectors, and enforcers. As Henry Hill confesses in voice-over at the beginning of *Goodfellas*,

> To me, being a gangster was better than being President of the United States. ... Even before I first wandered into the cabstand for an after-school job, I knew I wanted to be part of them. It was there that I knew I belonged. To me, it meant being somebody in a neighborhood that was full of nobodies. They weren't like anybody else. I mean, they did whatever they wanted. They double-parked in front of a hydrant and nobody gave them a ticket. In the summer when they played cards all night, nobody ever called the cops.

This materialistic allure of gangster life where you can get what you want is motivated primarily in Scorsese films by the Sicilian concept of *rispetto* ('respect'). It is the ultimate achievement for the gangster and can be seen as a combination of 'love, fear, loyalty, and duty toward the family order' (Casillo 2007: 89). This respect is central to the gangster's outlook of success and the wise guy's relationship to the community. As Casillo notes, 'the Italian American mob plays an important unofficial and clandestine role in the community, as its leaders not only help to maintain peace but, as men of honour and power, gain respect in doing so. The social drama of *rispetto* unfolds every day on the neighborhood streets, in the constant show of honour and deference among individuals and families' (2007:

'You look like a gangster!' Young Henry Hill dresses for success: *Goodfellas* (1990)

109). The quest to achieve and maintain this sense of honour is a central theme in Scorsee's wise guy trilogy.

Wise Guys, Goodfellas, and Gamblers

In 2002 Scorsese made a historical epic gangster film, *Gangs of New York,* that has been called 'a prequel to the entire Hollywood gangster genre' (Nochimson 2007: 211). Based on Herbert Asbury's chronicle of nineteenth-century New York City street gangs, it recounts the adventures of Irish immigrant Amsterdam Vallon (Leonardo DiCaprio) in the notorious Five Points district of New York City during the Civil War Draft Riots of 1863. Lording over the various Five Points gangs is the presence of Bill the Butcher (Daniel Day Lewis), a cutthroat gang leader who is in league with Tammany Hall in controlling the votes through physical coercion. The major conflict in the film arises from the opposition between the so-called nativists and the newly arrived immigrants – but within the historical context of the film New York is a polyphony of gangs that includes everyone – even the wealthy. The film, though not directly related to Scorsese's wise guy trilogy, is a further 'anthropological study' or, perhaps more appropriately, an archeological study of the origins of the urban street gangs who fought essentially for survival of the fittest in the early history of American industrialization. Martha Nochimson notes that Scorsese 'plunges the genre into a nineteenth-century context that makes available an unusually raw, direct connection between immigration and the gangster through a saga of striving and desire in the shadow of the Civil War' (2007: 206).

Scorsese's wise guy trilogy can also be viewed as a chronological study of the development of the gangs from their street-wise origins in contemporary New York to their ill-fated attempt at adoption of a business-like bureaucracy in Las Vegas. As Casillo notes, the films that make up this 'trilogy'

> eschew a mythifying treatment of Italian American criminals in favour of a disturbingly realistic presentation clearly reflecting the vicissitudes of Italian America. ... Scorsese's gangster films depict not only the disintegration of the ethnic community through intermarriage and transplantation, but the deterioration of the mob through increased police surveillance, betrayals, and corporate competition. (2007: 180)

This realism of the dissolution of ethnicity often focuses on the loss of respect as the Italian American gangster is further displaced through his assimilation into American culture.

Mean Streets was Scorsese's initial gangster film and its naturalistic visual style contributes to the demythologization of the gangster through Charlie's relationship with his Uncle Giovanni (Cesare Danova). Charlie (through his confessional voice-over narration – supplied at times by Scorsese himself) is conflicted between his devout Catholicism and his opportunity to advance in the local Mafia through Giovanni, the neighborhood mob boss. Charlie works for his uncle as a debt collector in the protection rackets throughout the neighborhood in Little Italy. Giovanni is a man of respect, who commands authority primarily through silence and his sage advice. When told that a restaurant owner cannot make his payments he asks Giovanni what to do and Giovanni says, 'Don't do anything. His business is bad.' This is a far cry from the physical strong-arm tactics typically displayed in mob films and is more realistic in terms of *rispetto* that the Mafioso acquires in his community. Part of Giovanni's idea of *rispetto* can be seen in his admiration for 'Lucky' Luciano, who he considers as an admirable 'man of honor' by virtue of the US government's use of him to maintain security in the New York docks during World

War II. Luciano's presence alone was all that was needed to maintain that security, according to Giovanni: 'He was there – that's what he did.' This mafiioso mystique is also displayed by Giovanni's presence, as he punctuates everything with his thin cigar, an emblem of authority and respect in the Italian community. Charlie's association with Johnny Boy ('he's half crazy') and his intimate relationship to Johnny's epileptic cousin, Teresa ('she's sick in the head'), troubles Giovanni. At one point he tells Charlie that 'honorable men go with honorable men', and he views Charlie's relationships as a weakness of his character. Indeed, it is Charlie's friendship with Johnny Boy that provides the basic dramatic conflict as well as the violent action in the film.

Johnny Boy is the irreverent prankster who is disrespectful of authority figures, even the US Government. Early in the film, he nonchalantly places an explosive device of some type into a corner mailbox, and laughs when it finally explodes scattering smoke and pieces of mail everywhere. Johnny is continually in debt to local loan sharks and refuses to pay, even as he buys drinks for one who is asking him for payment. It is Charlie's relationship with Johnny Boy that is of particular concern to Giovanni, who sees him as simple crazy; and it is this relationship that prevents Charlie from advancing in the local Mafia. Fran Mason sees Charlie as an interface between the established mob and the 'wannabe gangsters' such as Johnny Boy – but as an interface he is an outsider in both realms. The outsider status is prevalent throughout the wise guy trilogy and is personified through such characters as Henry Hill in *Goodfellas* and 'Ace' Rothstein in *Casino*. The outsider figure always attempts to become a part of the gang but is conflicted in some way through personal desires or through his association with trickster figures. Likewise, in each film the outsider is provided with a business enterprise by the gang as a way of assimilation into the mob as well as into American culture. In *Mean Streets* Uncle Giovanni wants to allow Charlie to take over the restaurant business from Oscar; in *Goodfellas* Henry Hill is given the Bamboo Lounge; and in *Casino* 'Ace' Rothstein is provided with the Tangiers casino to help the mob establish itself in Las Vegas. In each the business ultimately fails through the outsider's friendship with potentially dangerous 'trickster' associates such as Johnny Boy, Tommy Devito (*Goodfellas*), and Nicky Santoro (*Casino*). Scorsese's use of the outsider gangster in his films allows for an examination of the seduction of mob life that motivates the outsider, and party of that seduction is the idea of *rispetto*.

Goodfellas advances the Italian-American gangster from the neighborhood of Little Italy to the metropolitan area of New York City, where the
local Mafioso, Paulie Cicero, controls the criminal activity through his protection racket. As Henry Hill states at one point,

> Hundreds of guys depended on Paulie and he got a piece of every-
> thing they made. It was tribute, just like in the old country, except
> they were doing it here in America. And all they got from Paulie
> was protection from other guys looking to rip them off. And that's
> what it is all about. That's what the FBI could never understand.
> That what Paulie and the organization does is offer protection for
> people who can't go to the cops. That's it. That's all it is. They're
> like the police department for wiseguys.

Paulie's status as Mafioso is significantly different from that of Don
Giovanni in *Mean Streets* and illustrates both his cultural assimilation and
his displacement.

The Black Gangster Tradition

The criminal representation of African-Americans in American film presents
another aspect of ethnic identity in the gangster film. As Jonathan Munby
suggests, black gangster films present 'a seditious site in the struggle for
self-representation against iniquitous and prejudicial forces' (1999: 225). It
is within this site of representation that the black gangster film dramatizes
the struggle with authority and his marginalized status within such cycles
as the race film, blaxploitation, and the hood films. This can apply equally
well to other ethnic criminal representations such as the Jewish gangster
(*Once Upon a Time in America*), Irish-American gangsters (*Public Enemy,
Angels With Dirty Faces* (1938)), and Chinese gangsters (*The Hatchet Man*
(1932)) with groups who have been historically marginalised in American
society.[5] The gangster image in American cinema has provided a means
of representation in conflict with the dominant society through criminal
enterprise.

Three distinct phases of black-oriented gangster films emerge that
'imaginatively present the cultural beliefs and social experiences of black

audiences during a particular time and place' (Reid 1993: 154). The 'race' films of the 1930s and 1940s sound era that were patterned after stand-ardized generic conventions; the blaxploitation cycle of the 1970s that featured black criminal anti-heroes; and the 'hood' films of the 1990s that focused on inner city problems and urban gun violence – these film cycles contributed to the depiction and development of a black centric gangster film tradition that reflected social problems and urban conditions apart from their mainstream Hollywood counterparts.

Black gangsters in race films primarily were involved in such criminal enterprises as policy and lottery gambling (i.e. the numbers racket) and the exploitation of legitimate businesses by 'protection'. In many cases this reflects historical black organized crime activities in urban centres such as New York City during the 1920s and 1930s.[6] Race films prolifer-ated during the Classical Hollywood era and were produced, distributed, and exhibited for black segregated audiences. Consequently, these films, according to Jonathan Munby, 'put black actors into roles that mainstream cinema denied them and dramatized aspects of the black experience that were given no representation on the white screen' (2005: 264). In some way race films, which comprised many genres including the western, the musical, and the gangster film, can be viewed as a counter-cinema where ethnic values and representation were foregrounded for their audiences (much like Yiddish films of the same period). The black screen gangster in race films can be seen as a reflection of the black urban experience during the Depression years, primarily through their representation of segregated black communities, their use of vaudeville humour, and black music.

Both Mark Reid (2003) and Jonathan Munby (2005) emphasize the importance of African-American film director and actor Ralph Cooper in developing the 'northern, urbanized black-gangster film stryle' (Reid 1993: 144) in the late 1930s. Cooper, a former song-and-dance-man and emcee for Harlem's Apollo Theatre, had a brief film career in Hollywood and was able to direct and star in several black-gangster race films including *Dark Manhattan* (1937), *Bargain with Bullets* (1937), *Gang War* (1940) and *Am I Guilty* (1940). As Munby notes, Cooper's black gangster films 'communi-cated the meaning of the gangster from a distinctively metropolitan and necessarily theatrical black perspective' (2005: 269). In 1941, Cooper quit making films and returned to his theatrical roots as emcee of the Apollo Theatre. However, the race gangster films that he made (as well as the ones made by his contemporary Oscar Micheaux) created a means of expressing the black underworld experience on film that would later be embellished by the blaxploitation cycle of the 1970s and the hood films of the 1990s.

Notes

1   These statistical findings were part of an Image Research Project conducted by the Italic Institute of America and can be found at the following web site: http//:italic.org/mediaWatch/filmstudy.
2   Syndicate films for example often portrayed gangsters as WASPish-like businessmen who were indistinguishable in appearance than the rest of society. Note the appearance of Otto Kruger in *711 Ocean Drive* (1950) or Edward Arnold and Alan Napier in *Miami Exposé* (1956). An even more prescient example is Robert Ryan in the Howard Hughes remake of *The Racket* (1951) whose gangster character name is changed from its original, Nick Scarsi, to Nick Scanlon.
3   Reliable historical sources on the Black Hand can be found in Thomas Monroe Pitkin and Francesco Cordasco (1977) *The Black Hand: A Chapter in Ethnic Crime*. Totawa, NJ: Littlefield, Adams and David Critchley (2009) *The Origin of Organized Crime in America: The New York City Mafia, 1891–1931*. New York and London: Routledge.
4   Another indication of the influence of Wellman's film on Scorsese is through his visual approach to the material. *The Public Enemy* is almost documentary-like in nature through its photographic realism and its use of titled inserts and montage sequences to note its historicity. For more on the film as history see J.E. Smyth (2010) 'Revisioning modern American history in the age of *Scarface* (1932)', *The Historical Journal of Film, Radio and Television*, 24, 4, 535–63.
5   For more nuanced and detailed readings of these ethnic gangster representations see Terry Barr (1999) 'Fagin's Children: Hollywood's Jewish Gangsters', *Studies in Popular Culture*, 22, 2, 71–84; Christopher Shannon (2005) 'Public Enemies, Local Heroes: The Irish-American Gangster Film in Classical Hollywood Cinema', *New Hibernia Review*, 9, 4, 48–64; and Peter Stanfield (2005) '"American as Chop Suey": Invocations of Gangsters in Chinatown, 1920–1936', in Lee Grieveson, Esther Sonnet, and Peter Stanfield (eds) *Mob Culture: Hidden Histories of the American Gangster Film*. New Brunswick, NJ: Rutgers University

Press: 238–62.

6   For more information concerning the history of black organized crime during the Depression-era, see Rufus Schatzberg and Robert J. Kelly (1997) *African American Organized Crime: A Social History.* New Brunswick, NJ: Rutgers University Press, and *Black Gangs of Harlem: 1920–1939* by Walter A Bell; online at http://www.crimelibrary.com/ gangsters_outlaws/gang/harlem_gangs/index.html.

CONCLUSION

The contemporary gangster film is best characterized by two main production tendencies: the historic and the contemporaneous. Both tendencies are further fragmented by their generic mobility as hybrids and sub-genres. The 1990s witnessed an upsurge in the production of gangster films with the year 1990 alone seeing the release of *Miller's Crossing* (Coen Brothers), *Goodfellas* (Martin Scorsese), *King of New York* (Abel Ferrara), and *The Godfather, Part III* (Francis Ford Coppola). Further developments in the 1990s include the gangsta hood cycle, the postmodern gangster films of Quentin Tarantino, and Russian Mafia films. Fran Mason claims that the gangster and the genre became polyvalent during this period within cross-generic signification as the gangster film blurred generic boundaries into the action-adventure high concept Hollywood film (2002: 146). Although Mason connects this polyvalence to postmodernity in assessing what were then contemporary gangster films, it is still distinguished in such films such as *Public Enemies* (2009) and *Killing Them Softly* (2012) and is further distinguished by technological developments such as the use of digital technology and the new editing practices that create what David Bordwell calls 'intensified continuity' (2002). By noting two primary tendencies it becomes easier to trace how the contemporary gangster genre is further fragmented and yet remains clearly identifiable as a gangster film through its reliance on the genre's historic development and its close connection to the topicality of true crime narratives. This, in turn, permits an examination of how filmmakers utilize certain conventions of the genre either stylistically or realistically to reflect historic or contemporary concerns. Mason asserts that 'contemporary gangster films can be studied in the types of strategy they utilize either to continue or problematise [their] tradition' (2002: 147). These strategies can be applied to the two tendencies discussed below.

The historic tendency is influenced by the classic gangster cycle of the early 1930s in its subject matter (real-life gangsters) and genre narrative conventions (cops-and-robbers, rise-and-fall structures). These films often focus on the exploits of a historic gangster figure and are presented as historically-based films through their period costuming, props, and art direction. The historic gangster tendency relies heavily on conventional narrative tropes of the classic gangster film that is embellished with a more action-driven stylistic. Typically high-concept Hollywood films, they also employ an 'intensified continuity' visual style to reflect their action-oriented narrative structure. This narrative structure is also evidenced in the prevalence of the cops-and-robbers formula in many of the films, such as *Public Enemies*, *American Gangster* (2007), and *Gangster Squad* (2013). The cops-and-robbers form allows for more intensely choreographed action sequences and dramatic confrontations that is also a standard narrative convention of many classical and post-classical gangster films. In contemporary historic gangster films these action sequences become more stylized and hyper-realistic through their use of screen violence. Martin Scorsese's *Gangs of New York* is also indicative of this tendency because of its high-concept depiction of the pre-modern history of the gangster figure in nineteenth-century America, and can be seen in many ways as a pre-cursor to the Progressive-era gangster films. The historic tendency in contemporary gangster films ultimately represents a re-conceptualization of the genre for modern audiences that rely on certain historical events combined with a contemporary visual style.

This visual style is characterized by rapid editing, close framing of dialogue sequences, a free ranging camera that seems to be in continual motion, and the use of a long-focus lens that exploits the extremes of lens length in the frame. According to Bordwell, 'intensified continuity is traditional continuity amped up, raised to a higher pitch of emphasis' (2002: 16). He further claims that it is the dominant style of contemporary American mass-audience films. With regard to the contemporary historic gangster film this style creates an appeal to modern audiences for the subject matter of the film, which is often advertised as an action-adventure-style cops-and-robbers narrative, rather than a gangster biopic. The directors associated with select films – Ridley Scott (*American Gangster*), Michael Mann (*Public Enemies*) – are action directors working in a variety of genres. These films also rely on a male star or a pairing of male stars for their marketability. For example, *American Gangster* uses Denzel Washington and Russell Crowe, *Public Enemies*, Johnny Depp and Christian Bale, and *Gangster Squad*, Sean Penn and Ryan Gosling. The films effectively become star vehicles rather than gangster biographies.

The period aesthetic of the contemporary historic gangster film is often grounded in a pristine appearance that belies any sense of historical verisimilitude. Though it is presented as 1950s Los Angeles in *L.A. Confidential* (1997) or the 1930s Depression-era Midwest in *Public Enemies* it is a contemporary vision of those eras rendered in a contemporary style. According to Adam Gallimore, 'the clash of the period events and digital filmmaking [in the case of *Public Enemies*, but it also applies to *Gangster Squad*] exposes a set of inherent contradictions between the present and the past, the modern and the classical, and the contrast between the reality of historical events and the artifice of digital filmmaking' (2014: 17). The majority of these films concern historical events and persons, but they are now imbued with star quality and an intensified style that renders their subjects as ahistorical action figures rather than real-life subjects. *Public Enemies* is a perfect example as the film concerns John Dillinger, but it is Dillinger as played by Johnny Depp. So it becomes more a film starring Johnny Depp than a film about Dillinger. Compared to *Dillinger* (1945) with Lawrence Tierney and *Dillinger* (1973) with Warren Oates, *Public Enemies* is much more action-driven and that action is intensified through its digital filmmaking techniques. The contemporary historical gangster has also been transferred to the small screen with Terence Winter's *Boardwalk Empire* (HBO, 2010–14) based on the life and career of 'Nucky' Thompson and peopled with such real-life gangster figures as Arnold Rothstein, 'Lucky' Luciano, Meyer Lansky, and Al Capone. These gangsters are not portrayed as larger-than-life historicized figures but rather in the Scorsese manner (Scorsese is also Executive Producer for the series) as street hoodlums depicted early in their criminal careers.

Perhaps the most innovative of the contemporary trends in the gangster film is the contemporaneous tendency. These films are heavily influenced by neo-noir crime films in their visual style, settings, and characters. The contemporaneous gangster films also utilize contemporary settings and are often based on both fictional and non-fictional sources. The noir influence is apparent through the representation of the gangster figure as an alienated individual in an increasingly complex, globalized environment. This environment effectively renders the gangster protagonist or protagonists as an emasculated, impotent male in a corporate structure that has eviscerated his manhood. The narrative focus of these films is on crime and the criminals themselves who are often distinguished by their ineptness. One of the primary influences on the contemporary gangster film is Quentin Tarantino whose films often emphasise the banal dialogue of their postmodern protagonists and also feature hyperviolence as an arthouse aesthetic. Films that reflect this tendency include *Reservoir Dogs* (1992), *Pulp Fiction* (1994), *Ghost Dog: The Way of the Samurai* (2000), *The Departed*, and *Killing Them Softly*. There is also a current trend towards what has been referred to as the 'new individualism' in the contemporary gangster film that often indicates the protagonist needs to re-assert himself in a modern trans-global economy.

The best current example of this tendency is Andrew Dominick's *Killing Them Softly*, based on George V. Higgins novel, *Cogan's Trade* from 1974. The film was updated to 2008 post-Katrina New Orleans during the Presidential election of Barack Obama. It concerns a heist of a mob-controlled card-game and the dispensation of mob authority by enforcer Jackie Cogan (Brad Pitt). Atypical of the historic tendency this film is primarily conversation-driven, with extended dialogue sequences between and about characters. A complimentary to Dominik's previous film, *The Assassination of Jesse James by the Coward Robert Ford* (2007), the film continues the Canadian filmmaker's demythologization of American culture via the gangster film. Although the character of Cogan is the most conventionally centered as a seasoned veteran mob enforcer, the other gangster characterisations are far less stable. John Gandolfini portrays Mickey, another mob hit man that Cogan sub-contracts for the job. Mickey is a washed out, misanthropic alcoholic enforcer who is incapable of performing his task and is eventually set up by Cogan to be arrested by the police. Ray Liotta plays Markie Trattman, the man whose card game is robbed and who is suspected of planning the heist itself. Markie is innocent but suffers the consequences of his own earlier robbery of a mob card-game and its fatal consequences. Although, they are gangster characters in the mold of *Goodfellas*, they are far from being the self-assured, self-centered wise guys and are now simply vacuous, shells of their former selves. By contrast, Cogan epitomises the methodical, by-the-book enforcer who is able to seduce his victims into their own demise, by basically talking them into death. The film re-establishes the use of the gangster as a metaphor through its depiction of the corporatisation of the crime syndicate – where no one seems to know proper procedure and cost-saving devices, as well as micro-management have become high priority.

These two contemporary tendencies illustrate how the gangster film has remained popular and contemporary through its fragmentation into contemporary genres and use of modern digital technology. The gangster film remains a viable form of critique of American values in the twenty-first century and a means of critiquing the national and global structure of corporatisation.

FILMOGRAPHY

This filmography consists solely of theatrically released feature-length American gangster films. Film selections included either contain or feature a gangster protagonist, story, or setting. Since this volume argues that the American gangster genre was characterised by its generic fluidity, the filmography also includes motion pictures where gangster film conventions were combined with other genres such as the musical, the horror film, science fiction, and comedy. Dates provided are theatrical release dates.

A Bronx Tale (Robert De Niro, 1993)
A Bullet for Joey (Larry Buchanan, 1955)
A Free Soul (Clarence Brown, 1931)
A History of Violence (David Cronenberg, 2005)
A Slight Case of Murder (Lloyd Bacon, 1938)
Al Capone (Richard Wilson, 1959)
Alibi (Roland West, 1929)
All Through the Night (Vincent Sherman, 1942)
American Gangster (Ridley Scott, 2007)
Amazing Dr. Clitterhouse, The (Anatol Litvak, 1938)
Analyze This (Harold Ramis, 1999)
Angel on My Shoulder (Archie Mayo, 1946)
Angels with Dirty Faces (Michael Curtiz, 1938)
Asphalt Jungle, The (John Huston, 1950)
A Slight Case of Murder (Lloyd Bacon, 1938)

Baby Face Nelson (Don Siegel, 1957)
Beast of the City (Charles Brabin, 1932)
Big City, The (Tod Browning, 1928)
Big Combo, The (Joseph H. Lewis, 1955)
Big Heat, The (Fritz Lang, 1953)
Big Operator, The (Charles Haas, 1959)
Big Shot, The (Lewis Seiler, 1942)
Billy Bathgate (Robert Benton, 1991)
Black Caesar (Larry Cohen, 1973)
Black Friday (Arthur Lubin, 1940)
Black Hand. The: True Story of a Recent Occurrence in the Italian Quarter
    of New York (Wallace McCutcheon and/or Frank Marion, 1906)
Black Hand, The (Richard Thorpe, 1950)
Black Tuesday (Hugo Fregonese, 1954)
Blast of Silence (Allen Baron, 1961)
Blind Alley (Charles Vidor, 1939)
Blondie Johnson (Ray Enright, 1933)
Blood Money (Roland Brown, 1933)
Bloody Mama (Roger Corman, 1970)
Body and Soul (Robert Rossen, 1947)
Bonnie and Clyde (Arthur Penn, 1967)
Bonnie Parker Story, The (William Witney, 1958)
Born Reckless (John Ford, 1930)
Boss, The (Byron Haskin, 1956)
Boyz'n the Hood (John Singleton, 1991)
Broadway (Paul Fejos, 1929)
Broadway (William A. Seiter, 1942)
Brother Orchid (Lloyd Bacon, 1940)
Brotherhood. The (Martin Ritt, 1968)
Brothers Rico, The (Phil Karlson, 1957)
Bugsy (Barry Levinson, 1990)
Bullets or Ballots (William Keighley, 1936)
Bullets over Broadway (Woody Allen, 1994)

Captive City (Robert Wise, 1952)
Carlito's Way (Brian De Palma, 1993)
Case Against Brooklyn, The (Paul Wendkos, 1958)

Casino (Martin Scorsese, 1995)
Charley Varrick (Don Siegel, 1973)
Chicago after Midnight (Ralph Ince, 1928)
Chicago Syndicate (Fred Sears, 1955)
Chicago Confidential (Sidney Salkow, 1957)
City Streets (Rouben Mamoullian, 1931)
Corsair (Roland West, 1932)
Cotton Club, The (Francis Ford Coppola, 1984)
Cotton Comes to Harlem (Ossie Davis, 1970)
Creature with the Atom Brain (Edward L. Cahn, 1955)
Crooked Way, The (Robert Florey, 1949)
Cry of the City (Robert Siodmak, 1948)
Czar of Broadway, The (William James Craft, 1930)

Damn Citizen (Robert Gordon, 1958)
Damned Don't Cry, The (Vincent Sherman, 1950)
Dance, Fools, Dance (Harry Beaumont, 1931)
Dark Past, The (Rudolph Mate, 1949)
Dead End (William Wyler, 1937)
Deadline U.S.A. (Richard Brooks, 1952)
Departed, The (Martin Scorsese, 2006)
Desperate Hours, The (William Wyler, 1955)
Diary of a Hitman (Roy London, 1992)
Dick Tracy (Warren Beatty, 1990)
Dillinger (Max Nosseck, 1945)
Dillinger (John Milius, 1973)
Doctor Socrates (William Dieterle, 1935)
Doorway to Hell, The (Archie Mayo, 1930)
Don is Dead, The (Richard Fleischer, 1973)
Donnie Brasco (Mike Newell, 1997)
Dragnet, The (Josef von Sternberg, 1928)
Dragnet (Jack Webb, 1954)

Earl of Chicago (Richard Thorpe, 1940)
East of the River (Alfred E. Green, 1940)
Eight Men Out (John Sayles, 1988)
Enforcer, The (Bretaigne Windust/Raoul Walsh, 1951)

Fall Guy, The (A. Leslie Pierce, 1930)
Finger Man (Harold Schuster, 1955)
Finger Points, The (John Francis Dillon, 1931)
Force of Evil (Abraham Polonsky, 1948)
Friends of Eddie Coyle, The (Peter Yates, 1973)

G-Men (William Keighley, 1935)
Gangs of New York (Martin Scorsese, 2002)
Gangster, The (Gordon Wiles, 1947)
Garment Jungle, The (Vincent Sherman, 1957)
Gentleman's Fate (Mervyn LeRoy, 1931)
Ghost Dog: The Way of the Samurai (Jim Jarmusch, 2000)
Gilda (Charles Vidor, 1946)
Glass Key, The (Frank Tuttle, 1935)
Glass Key, The (Stuart Heisler, 1942)
Godfather, The (Francis Ford Coppola, 1972)
Godfather, Part II, The (Francis Ford Coppola, 1974)
Godfather, Part III, The (Francis Ford Coppola, 1990)
Grissom Gang, The (Robert Aldrich, 1971)
Guilty Generation, The (Rowland V. Lee, 1931)
Gun Crazy (Joseph H. Lewis, 1949)
Guys and Dolls (Joseph L. Mankiewicz, 1955)

Harder They Fall, The (Mark Robson, 1956)
Hatchet Man, The (William Wellman, 1932)
Hell on Frisco Bay (Frank Tuttle, 1956)
Hell Up in Harlem (Janelle Cohen, 1973)
Hickey and Boggs (Robert Culp, 1972)
High Sierra (Raoul Walsh, 1941)
Highway 301 (Andrew I. Stone, 1950)
His Kind of Woman (John Farrow, 1951)
Hoodlum, The (Max Nosseck, 1951)
Hoodlum Empire (Joseph Kane, 1952)
Hook, Line and Sinker (Edward F. Cline, 1930)
House of Bamboo (Sam Fuller, 1955)
Houston Story, The (William Castle, 1956)
Human Cargo (Allan Dwan, 1936)

Hush Money (Sidney Lanfield, 1931)

I Am the Law (Alexander Hall, 1938)
I Cover the Underworld (R.G. Springsteen, 1955)
I Cover the Waterfront (James Cruze, 1933)
I Died a Thousand Times (Stuart Heisler, 1955)
I, Mobster (Roger Corman, 1959)
I Walk Alone (Byron Haskins, 1948)
Illegal (Lewis Allen, 1955)
Illegal Traffic (Louis King, 1938)
Inside Detroit (Fred F. Sears, 1955)
Inside the Mafia (Edward L. Cahn, 1959)
Intolerance (The Modern Story) (D.W. Griffith, 1916)

Joe Macbeth (Ken Hughes, 1955)
Johnny Allegro (Ted Tetzlaff, 1949)
Johnny Apollo (Henry Hathaway, 1940)
Johnny Eager (Mervyn LeRoy, 1942)

Kansas City Confidential (Phil Karlson, 1952)
Key Largo (John Huston, 1948)
Kid Galahad (Michael Curtiz, 1937)
Killers, The (Robert Siodmak, 1946)
Killers, The (Don Siegel, 1964)
Killing, The (Stanley Kubrick, 1956)
Killing of a Chinese Bookie, The (John Cassavetes, 1976)
Killing Them Softly (Andrew Dominik, 2012)
King of the Roaring Twenties: The Story of Arnold Rothstein (Joseph M.
    Newman, 1961)
King of the Underworld (Lewis Seiler, 1939)
Kiss of Death (Henry Hathaway, 1947)
Kiss Tomorrow Goodbye (Gordon Douglas, 1950)

Lady Scarface (Frank Woodruff, 1941)
Lady Killer (Roy Del Ruth, 1933)
Larceny Inc. (Lloyd Bacon, 1942)
Last Gangster, The (Edward Ludwing, 1937)

Lepke (Menachim Golan, 1975)
Let 'Em Have It (Sam Wood, 1935)
Lights of New York (Bryan Foy, 1928)
Lineup, The (Don Siegel, 1958)
Little Caesar (Mervyn LeRoy, 1931)
Little Giant (Roy Del Ruth, 1933)
Loan Shark (Seymour Friedman, 1952)
Love Me or Leave Me (Charles Vidor, 1955)
Love That Brute (Alexander Hall, 1950)
Lucky Jordan (Frank Tuttle, 1942)
Lucky Luciano (Francesco Rosi, 1974)

Ma Barker's Killer Brood (Bill Karan, 1960)
Machine Gun Kelly (Roger Corman, 1958)
Mack, The (Michael Campus, 1973)
Manhattan Melodrama (W.S. Van Dyke, 1934)
Marked Woman (Lloyd Bacon, 1937)
Married to the Mob (Jonathan Demme, 1988)
Me, Gangster (Raoul Walsh, 1928)
Mean Streets (Martin Scorsese, 1973)
Mechanic, The (Michael Winner, 1972)
Menace II Society (The Hughes Brothers, 1993)
Men Without Names (Ralph Murphy, 1935)
Miami Expose (Fred F. Sears, 1956)
Miami Story, The (Fred F. Sears, 1954)
Miller's Crossing (Joel Cohen, 1990)
Mob, The (Robert Parrish, 1951)
Mouthpiece, The (James Flood, Elliott Nugent, 1932)
Murder by Contract (Irving Lerner, 1958)
Murder, Inc. (Burt Balaban/Stuart Rosenberg, 1960)
Musketeers of Pig Alley, The (D.W. Griffith, 1912)
My Blue Heaven (Herbert Ross, 1990)

New Jack City (Mario Van Peebles, 1991)
New York Confidential (Russell Rouse, 1955)
Nickel Ride, The (Robert Mulligan, 1974)

Once Upon a Time in America (Sergio Leone, 1984)
On the Waterfront (Elia Kazan, 1954)
Out of the Fog (Anatole Litvak, 1941)
Out of the Past (Jacques Tourneur, 1947)
Outfit, The (John Flynn, 1973)

Party Girl (Nicholas Ray, 1958)
Payback (Brian Helgeland, 1999)
Pay or Die! (Richard Wilson, 1960)
Penthouse (W. S. Van Dyke, 1933)
Pete Kelly's Blues (Jack Webb, 1955)
Petrified Forest, The (Archie Mayo, 1936)
Phenix City Story, The (Phil Karlson, 1955)
Point Blank (John Boorman, 1967)
Portrait of a Mobster (Joseph Pevney, 1961)
Pretty Boy Floyd (Herbert J. Leder, 1961)
Prizzi's Honor (John Huston, 1985)
Public Enemy (William Wellman, 1931)
Public Enemy's Wife (Nick Grinde, 1936)
Public Enemies (Michael Mann, 2009)
Public Hero #1 (J. Walter Ruben, 1935)
Pulp Fiction (Quentin Tarantino, 1994)
Purple Gang, The (Frank McDonald, 1959)

Queen of the Mob (James Hogan, 1940)
Quick Millions (Rowland Brown, 1931)

Racket, The (Lewis Milestone, 1928)
Racket, The (John Cromwell, 1951)
Racket Busters (Lloyd Bacon, 1938)
Regeneration (Raoul Walsh, 1915)
Reservoir Dogs (Quentin Tarantino, 1992)
Rise and Fall of Legs Diamond, The (Bud Boetticher, 1961)
Road to Perdition, The (Sam Mendes, 2002)
Roaring Twenties, The (Raoul Walsh, 1939)
Roger Toughy, Gangster! (Robert Florey, 1944)
Rubber Racketeers (Harold Young, 1942)

Scarface (Howard Hawks, 1932)
Scarface (Brian de Palma, 1983)
Scarface Mob, The (Phil Karlson, 1960)
Secret Six, The (George Hill, 1931)
Show Them No Mercy (George Marshall, 1935)
Smart Money (Alfred E. Green, 1931)
Smashing the Rackets (Lew Landers, 1938)
Some Like it Hot (Billy Wilder, 1959)
St. Valentine's Day Massacre, The (Roger Corman, 1967)
Star Witness, The (William Wellman, 1931)
Stop, You're Killing Me (Roy Del Ruth, 1952)
Story of Temple Drake, The (Stephen Roberts, 1933)

T-Men (Anthony Mann, 1947)
Taxi! (Roy Del Ruth, 1932)
This Day and Age (Cecil B. DeMille, 1933)
Three on a Match (Mervyn LeRoy, 1932)
Thunderbolt (Josef Von Sternberg, 1929)
Tight Spot (Phil Karlson, 1955)
Tough Guys (Jeff Kanew, 1986)
True Romance (Tony Scott, 1993)

Undercover Man, The (Joseph H. Lewis, 1949)
Underworld (Josef von Sternberg, 1927)
Underworld U.S.A. (Sam Fuller, 1961)
Unholy Three, The (Tod Browning, 1925)
Unholy Three, The (Jack Conway, 1930)
Untouchables, The (Brian de Palma, 1987)

Valachi Papers, The (Terence Young, 1972)
Voices of the City (Wallace Worsley, 1921)
Voice of the City (Willard Mack, 1929)

Weary River (Frank Lloyd, 1929)
When Gangland Strikes (R.G. Springsteen, 1956)
White Heat (Raoul Walsh, 1948)
Whole Town's Talking, The (John Ford, 1935)

Widow from Chicago, The (Edward Cline, 1930)
Wise Guys (Brian de Palma, 1986)

Yakuza, The (Sidney Pollack, 1975)
You and Me (Fritz Lang, 1938)
You Only Live Once (Fritz Lang, 1937)
Young Dillinger (Terry O. Morse, 1965)

BIBLIOGRAPHY

Altman, Rick (1999) *Film/Genre*. London: British Film Institute.

Anderson, Christopher (1994) *HollywoodTV: The Studio System in the Fifties*. Austin, TX: University of Texas Press.

Barnouw, Eric (1977) *Tube of Plenty: The Evolution of American Television*. New York: Oxford University Press.

Basinger, Jeanine (1999) *Silent Stars*. New York: Alfred A. Knopf.

Baxter, John (1970) *The Gangster Film*. New York: A.S. Barnes.

Behlmer, Rudy (1985) *Inside Warner Bros., 1935–1951*. New York: Viking Penguin.

Bergman, Andrew (1992) *We're in the Money: Depression America and Its Films*. Chicago: Elephant Paperbacks.

Bernstein, Lee (2002) *The Greatest Menace: Organized Crime in Cold War America*. Amherst, MA: University of Massachusetts Press.

Betz, Mark (2008) 'Little Books' in Lee Grieveson and Haidee Wasson (eds) *Inventing Film Studies*. Durham, NC: Duke University Press, 319–49.

Biesen, Sheri Chinen (2005) *Blackout: World War II and the Origins of Film Noir*. Baltimore, MD: Johns Hopkins University Press.

Bondanella, Peter (2004) *Hollywood Italians*. New York: Continuum.

Bordwell, David (2002) 'Intensified Continuity: Visual Style in Contemporary American Film', *Film Quarterly*, 55, 3, 16–28.

Breu, Christopher (2005) *Hard-Boiled Masculinities*. Minneapolis: University of Minnesota Press.

Browne, Nick (ed.) (1999) *Francis Ford Coppola's The Godfather Trilogy*. New York: Cambridge University Press.

Camon, Alessandro (2000) '*The Godfather* and the Mythology of the Mafia', in Nick Browne (ed.) *Franicis Ford Coppola's The Godfather Trilogy*. New York: Cambridge University Press, 57–75.

Casillo, Robert (2007) *Gangster Priest: The Italian American Cinema of Martin Scorsese*. Toronto: University of Toronto Press.

_____ (2012) 'Prelude to *The Godfather*: Martin Ritt's *The Brotherhood*', in Dana Renga (ed.) *Mafia Movies*. Toronto: University of Toronto Press, 85–93.

Christie, Ian and David Thompson (eds) (2003) *Scorsese on Scorsese*. London: Faber and Faber.

Clarens, Carlos (1980) *Crime Movies: An Illustrated History*. New York: W.W. Norton.

Cook, Pam (ed.) (1985) *The Cinema Book*. London: British Film Institute.

Cortes, Carlos E. (1987) 'Italian-Americans in Film: From Immigrants to Icons', *MELUS*, 14, 3, 107–26.

Crafton, Donald (1997) *The Talkies: American Cinema's Transition to Sound, 1926–1931*. Berkeley, CA: University of California Press.

Custen, George E. (1997) *Twentieth Century's Fox: Darryl F. Zanuck and the Culture of Hollywood*. New York: Basic Books.

Dika, Vera (2000) 'The Representation of Ethnicity in *The Godfather*', in Nick Browne (ed.) *Francis Ford Coppola's The Godfather Trilogy*. New York: Cambridge University Press, 76–107.

Forman, Henry James (1935) *Our Movie-Made Children*. New York: Macmillan.

Friedman, Lawrence (1997) *The Cinema of Martin Scorsese*. New York: Continuum.

Gabree, John (1973) *Gangsters: From Little Caesar to The Godfather*. New York: Pyramid.

Gallimore, Adam (2014) '"We Ain't Thinking About Tomorrow": Narrative Immediacy and the Digital Period Aesthetic in Michael Mann's *Public Enemies*", *Scope: An Online Journal of Film and Television Studies*, 26, February, 1–23.

Glancy, H. Mark (1995) 'Warner Bros. Film Grosses, 1921–51: The William Schaefer ledger', *Historical Journal of Film, Radio and Television*, 15, 1, 55–73.

Gledhill, Christine (1985) 'The gangster/crime film' in Pam Cook (ed.) *The Cinema Book*. London: British Film Institute, 85–92.

Gorman, John (1971) *Kefauver: A Political Biography*. New York: Oxford University Press.

Grant, Barry Keith (ed.) (1986) *Film Genre Reader*. Austin, TX: University of

Texas Press.

Grieveson, Lee (2005) 'Gangsters and Governance in the Silent Era', in Lee Grieveson, Esther Sonnet, and Peter Stanfield (eds) *Mob Culture: Hidden Histories of the American Gangster Film*. New Brunswick, NJ: Rutgers University Press, 13–40.

Grieveson, Lee, Esther Sonnet, and Peter Stanfield (eds) (2005) *Mob Culture: Hidden Histories of the American Gangster Film*. New Brunswick, NJ: Rutgers University Press.

Grieveson, Lee and Haidee Wasson (2008) *Inventing Film Studies*. Durham, NC: Duke University Press.

Hall, Mordaunt (1930) 'Gang "Wars" in New Film', *The New York Times*, 23 November.

Hays, Will (1934) Telegram, 20 March. MPPDA Digital Archive. Online. Available at: http://mppda.flinders.edu.au/records/991 (accessed 4 July 2014).

_____ (1935) Memo, 6 September. MPPDA Digital Archive. Online. Available at: http://mppda.flinde's.edu.au/records/2566 (accessed 4 July 2014)

Hillier, Jim (1985) *Cahiers du Cinema: The 1950s – Neo-Realism, Hollywood, New Wave*. Cambridge, MA: Harvard University Press.

Hobsbawm, Eric (2000) *Bandits*. New York: New Press.

Jacobs, Lea (2008) *The Decline of Sentiment: American Film in the 1920s*. Berkeley, CA: University of California Press.

Kefauver, Estes (1951) 'Crime in America and its Effects on Foreign Relations', *Vital Speeches*, 17: 21 (August 15).

Kendrick, James (2009) *Film Violence: History, Ideology, Genre*. London and New York: Wallflower Press.

Kozloff, Sarah (1988) *Invisible Storytellers: Voice-Over Narration in the American Fiction Film*. Berkeley, CA: University of California Press.

_____ (2000) *Overhearing Film Dialogue*. Berkeley, CA: University of California Press.

Krutnik, Frank (1991) *In a Lonely Street: Film Noir, Genre, Masculinity*. New York: Routledge.

Leitch, Thomas (2002) *Crime Films*. Cambridge: Cambridge University Press.

Maggitti, Vinceno (2011) 'Wallace McCutcheon's *The Black Hand*: A Different Version of a Biograph Kidnapping', in Dana Renga (ed.) *Mafia Movies:*

A Reader. Toronto: University of Toronto Press, 51–67.

Maltby, Richard (1993) 'The Production Code and the Hays Office', in Tino Balio (ed.) *Grand Design: Hollywood as a Modern Business Enterprise, 1930–1939*. Berkeley, CA: University of California Press, 37–72.

____ (2001) 'The Spectacle of Criminality', in J. David Slocum (ed.) *Violence and American Cinema*. New York: Routledge, 117–52.

____ (2005) 'Why Boys Go Wrong: Gangsters, Hoodlums, and the Natural History of Delinquent Careers', in Lee Grieveson, Esther Sonnet, and Peter Stanfield (eds) *Mob Culture: Hidden Histories of the American Gangster Film*. New Brunswick, NJ: Rutgers University Press, 41–66.

Mason, Fran (2002) *American Gangster Cinema: From Little Caesar to Pulp Fiction*. New York: Palgrave Macmillan.

Mayo, Morrow (1931) 'Glorifying the Criminal', *The Commonweal*, September 9: 438–9.

McArthur, Colin (1972) *Underworld U.S.A.* London: Secker and Warburg.

McGilligan, Pat (1986) *Backstory: Interviews with Screenwriters from Hollywood's Golden Age*. Berkeley, CA: University of California Press.

Mitchell, Edward (1986) 'Apes and Essences: Sources of Significance in the American Gangster Film', in Barry Keith Grant (ed.) *Film Genre Reader*. Austin, TX: University of Texas Press, 159–67.

Munby, Jonathan (1999) *Public Enemies, Public Heroes: Screening the Gangster from Little Caesar to Touch of Evil*. Chicago: University of Chicago Press.

____ (2005) 'The Underworld Films of Oscar Micheaux and Ralph Cooper: Towards a Genealogy of the Black Screen Gangster', in Lee Grieveson, Esther Sonnet, and Peter Stanfield (eds) *Mob Culture: Hidden Histories of the American Gangster Film*. New Brunswick, NJ: Rutgers University Press, 263–80.

Neale, Steve (2000) *Genre and Hollywood*. London and New York: Routledge.

Nebel, Frederick (2007) 'The Crimes of Richmond City', in Otto Penzler (ed.) *The Black Lizard Big Book of Pulps*. New York: Vintage Books, 657–763.

Nochimson, Martha (2007) *Dying to Belong: Gangster Movies in Hollywood and Hong Kong*. Oxford: Blackwell.

Osgerby, Bill and Anna Gough-Yates (2001) *Action TV: Tough Guys, Smooth Operators, and Foxy Chics*. New York: Routledge Press.

Peary, Gerald (ed.) (1981) *Little Caesar*. Madison: University of Wisconsin Press.

Pelizzon, Penelope V. and Nancy M. West (2010) *Tabloid, Inc.: Crimes, Newspapers, Narratives*. Columbus: Ohio State University Press.

Penzler, Otto (ed.) (2007) *The Black Lizard Big Book of Pulps*. New York: Vintage Books.

Reid, Mark A. (1993) 'The Black Gangster Film', *Journal of Social Philosophy*, 24, 3, 143–54.

Renga, Dana (ed.) (2011) *Mafia Movies: A Reader*. Toronto: University of Toronto Press.

Riis, Jacob (2010 [1890]) *How the Other Half Lives*. New York: W.W. Norton.

Roddick, Nick (1983) *A New Deal in Entertainment: Warner Brothers in the 1930s*. London: British Film Institute.

Rosow, Eugene (1978) *Born to Lose: The Gangster Film in America*. New York: Oxford University Press.

Russo, John Paul (2011) 'Thematic Patterns in Francis Ford Coppola's *The Godfather, Part II*', in Dana Renga (ed.) *Mafia Movies: A Reader*. Toronto: University of Toronto Press, 111–17.

Ruth, David E. (1996) *Inventing the Public Enemy: The Gangster in American Culture, 1918–1934*. Chicago: University of Chicago Press.

Sante, Luc (1991) *Low Life*. New York: Farrar, Strauss, Giroux.

Santopietro, Tom (2012) *The Godfather Effect*. New York: St. Martin's Press.

Schatz, Thomas (1981) *Hollywood Genres: Formulas, Filmmaking, and the Studio System*. New York: McGraw-Hill.

Sennwald, André (1935) 'Public Hero No. 1', *The New York Times*, 8 June, 12.

Shadoian, Jack (2003 [1977]) *Dreams and Dead Ends: The American Gangster Film*, revised edition. New York: Oxford University Press.

Sklar, Robert (1992) *City Boys*. Princeton, NJ: Princeton University Press.

Smith, Erin A. (2000) *Hard Boiled: Working-Class Readers and Pulp Magazines*. Philadelphia: Temple University Press.

Smyth, J.E. (2010) 'Revisioning modern American history in the age of *Scarface* (1932)', *The Historical Journal of Film, Radio and Television*, 24, 4, 535–63.

Spicer, Andrew (2002) *Film Noir*. New York: Longman

Stanfield, Peter (2010) 'Punks!: Topicality and the 1950s Gangster Bio-Pic

Cycle', in Kingsley Bolton and Jan Olsson (eds) *Media, Popular Culture, and the American Century*. Bloomington, IN: Indiana University Press, 185–215.

Straw, Will (1997) 'Urban Confidential: The Lurid City of the 1950s', in David B. Clarke (ed.) *The Cinematic City* edited by. New York: Routledge, 113–30.

Thompson, Frank (1995) *Robert Wise: A Bio-Bibliography*. Westport, CT: Greenwood Press.

Thompson, Kirsten Moana (2007) *Crime Films*. London and New York: Wallflower Press.

Usai, Paolo Cherchi (2002) *The Griffith Project: Films Produced in 1912, Volume VI*. London: British Film Institute.

Vahimagi, Tise (1998) *The Untouchables*. London: British Film Institute.

Variety (1952) '*Hoodlum Empire*', 20 February, 6.

Warshow, Robert (1962 [1948]) 'The Gangster as Tragic Hero', in *The Immediate Experience: Movies, Comics, Theatre and Other Aspects of Popular Culture*. New York: Atheneum, 127–33.

Weiler, A. H. (1952) '*Hoodlum Empire*', *The New York Times*, 6 March, 25.

INDEX